Work It Out!

HOW TO FIND THE WORK
YOU ALWAYS WANTED IN A
SHIFTING JOBS MARKET

DES McCABE

HAY
HOUSE

HAY HOUSE

Australia • Canada • Hong Kong • India
South Africa • United Kingdom • United States

First published and distributed in the United Kingdom by:
Hay House UK Ltd, 62 1230;

Published and distributed in the United States of America by:
Hay House, Inc., 431 7695
or (800) 654 5126 ouse.com

Published and distributed in Australia by:
Hay House Australia Ltd, 18/36 Ralph St, Alexandria NSW 2015.
Tel.: (61) 2 9669 4299; Fax: (61) 2 9669 4144. www.hayhouse.com.au

Published and distributed in the Republic of South Africa by:
Hay House SA (Pty), Ltd, PO Box 990, Witkoppen 2068.
Tel./Fax: (27) 11 467 8904. www.hayhouse.co.za

Published and distributed in India by:
Hay House Publishers India, Muskaan Complex, Plot No.3, B-2, Vasant Kunj,
New Delhi – 110 070. Tel.: (91) 11 4176 1620; Fax: (91) 11 4176 1630.
www.hayhouse.co.in

Distributed in Canada by:
Raincoast, 9050 Shaughnessy St, Vancouver, BC V6P 6E5.
Tel.: (1) 604 323 7100; Fax: (1) 604 323 2600

© Des McCabe, 2011

The moral rights of the author have been asserted.

The author of this book does not dispense medical advice or prescribe the use of any technique as a form of treatment for physical or medical problems without the advice of a physician, either directly or indirectly. The intent of the author is only to offer information of a general nature to help you in your quest for emotional and spiritual wellbeing. In the event you use any of the information in this book for yourself, which is your constitutional right, the author and the publisher assume no responsibility for your actions.

A catalogue record for this book is available from the British Library.

ISBN 978-1-84850-464-6

Printed and bound in Great Britain by
TJ International, Padstow, Cornwall.

MIX
Paper from
responsible sources
FSC® C013056

To Ma and Da, with love

Acknowledgements

With special thanks to Nuala Moran, Jimmy Ryan, Richard McQuillen, Joan Browne, Roger Wilson-Hinds, Damien Maddalena, Celine White and Pauline McCabe for their inspiration, expertise and support.

Contents

Introduction

Work It Out! is a new way to think about
your working life.

Looking at rising unemployment, the daily toll of
redundancies and the squeeze on pensions, it's not
hard to spot that the traditional model of working full
time for a single employer, or starting a business and
being self-employed full time, is no longer a realistic
option for most of us. Work It Out! is the alternative
to devoting all your time to one job – often to the
exclusion of other interests. The Work It Out! approach
helps you to build a career out of individual 'pieces'
of work, put together and integrated with the other
aspects of your life.

Work It Out! is about far more than what you do to earn money. It provides a template for making work fit into your life, providing you with an income and financial security but also accommodating the needs of family and relationships, while also satisfying your personal ambitions.

Along with changing views of how work should be structured, Work It Out! addresses how we expect to be compensated. Of course we still need income, but the Work It Out! network makes it possible to barter skills and time, to be able to do volunteer work and to work at cost, for example as an investment in a joint piece of work.

Such 'workpieces' can include:

- paid or unpaid freelancing

- part-time working

- looking after children

- selling online

- temporary contracts

- caring for a sick friend or relative

- learning a new skill

- providing a service

- volunteering

- starting up new projects

- testing new business ideas.

You no longer have to sit and wait for someone to offer you a job. Work It Out! enables you to create your own set of workpieces and to change and adapt these over time.

THE ROLE OF THE INTERNET, POLICY-MAKERS AND EDUCATION

The Internet is playing a central role in the end of the traditional work model as we know it – but it also underpins the new world of work, enabling us to communicate and collaborate with fellow Work It Out! workers anywhere in the world, to create and fulfil workpieces.

Where once we cooperated with colleagues in the workplace, we can now use social networking sites to make connections, scope projects, find clients and deliver the goods.

Work It Out! also has important implications for policy-makers. In particular there is a need for governments to shift from supporting companies as the main tool of job-creation and start to invest in supporting individuals.

A good education will still help you to find work, but now education must encompass the skills of workpiece creation and collaboration – skills that last a lifetime.

THE END OF WORK AS WE KNOW IT

All this talk about 'the end of work' may seem gloomy – after all, although there is a recession at the moment, won't it end at some point? Well, yes, but not before employers have glimpsed the flexibility, lower cost base and productivity gains they can derive when they no longer package up the work that needs to be done into full-time jobs. Given the support of a Work It Out! network, employers will be able to establish exactly the skills and amount of time that they need, when they need it. It's a totally new model of human resourcing – featuring lots of very focused tasks rather than a few jobs, and creating opportunities for Work It Out! workers.

In this scenario, unemployment schemes are no longer just about keeping people off the unemployment register. Work It Out! initiatives for those who are out of work can actually offer real hope, encouragement and practical help. They are a springboard for creating and supporting new careers. A community project with a Government allowance can become an individual's first workpiece, allowing him or her to build from there.

Work It Out! is already a reality. Given round-the-clock Internet access from mobiles and computers, it is now possible to manage all our different activities seamlessly from home, in transit or from an office. The Internet provides the platform and resources to plan, develop and execute workpieces, and for each of us to become self-sufficient.

CHAPTER 1

The New World of Work

The old realities of the job market have been swept aside by globalization, outsourcing, the Internet and, now, the economic crisis. This is putting a new spin on the question, 'What do you want to be when you grow up?' Even worse, the assumption that if you study hard you will get the job of your dreams is no longer guaranteed. Work It Out! is a template for putting together a collection of 'workpieces' – some paid, some not – to provide financial independence while improving the balance between your work and the other aspects of your life.

WHAT WOULD YOU REALLY LIKE TO DO?

'I've just had the worst day of my life,' was the answer I got when I asked the upset young woman sitting across from me if she was OK. It was the last train from Belfast to Dublin and Mary was on her way to a job interview the next day. 'I've just failed my driving test and got yet another "No" to a job application. Who waits until they're 24 to take their driving test?' she said, chastising herself. 'I'm probably wasting my time going to Dublin for this interview.'

Mary is a Marketing graduate who should know all about promoting herself in an increasingly competitive job market. This was more than a 'bad day'. She was weary from all the rejections and disappointments, and clearly in no frame of mind to impress a potential employer. For Mary the upcoming interview was not an opportunity to display her talents, but rather another painful step in the process of trying to find a job. Financial pressures had forced her back home to live with her parents in Belfast, and Mary was desperate to get work.

It was when I asked her, 'What would you really like to do?' that Mary looked up and her eyes engaged me properly for the first time. With a nervous half-smile, she told me that her ambition was to open a clothes shop for older women. Mary knew exactly what the shop would sell and where it would be located. We chatted about how she could do something now to start to make this a reality – find out what older women in the area really wanted, identify gaps in the market, assess the competition, identify potential designers and suppliers, and so on. Basic research and creating links were two priorities if Mary was ever going to make her dream a reality. Her marketing brain started to kick in and she was buzzing.

It seems to me there is little point in dreams and ambition if we never act on them. What was Mary waiting for? She could continue to apply for jobs and re-sit her driving test – but now she had a project that needed some proper attention. Within a few minutes her whole attitude had changed. She saw she could take control of her own situation. Rather than being a passive cog, Mary could envision actions she could take to move forward.

The following morning I told this story to an enterprise specialist with responsibility for helping people to start up their own business. When I mentioned how asking Mary, 'What would you really like to do?' had provided such a spark, his expression changed. It was clear that no one had ever asked *him* the question, either. His body language told me that whatever he wanted to do, it certainly wasn't a government role trying to encourage people into self-employment. And he told me that many of his clients felt forced into going it alone because the job market had dried up. 'Reluctant entrepreneurs' is what he called them.

Our current world of work allows for only two options: sending out CVs in the hope of landing that elusive job, or starting your own business. Yes, there are courses to take and new qualifications to acquire, but that merely means being better qualified to compete in the same job market (and remember, too, it can be possible to be overqualified).

Now a third route is emerging; one that charts a different path. It's called Work It Out! and it involves developing different, discrete pieces of work and linking these together.

Before embarking on this path it is important to be able the answer the question, 'What would you really like to do? This provides the first step in the direction you should take. So ask yourself:

What would I really like to do?

1. ....

2. ....

3. ....

Keep these thoughts in mind as you are reading this book and thinking about your situation. As you get more ideas, write them down.

Thinking about what you want to do is the first step. Exactly how to go about achieving this – building income, developing a collection of workpieces and creating a sustainable career – is what this book is about.

STUDY HARD AND GET A GOOD JOB?

We have been brought up to believe studying hard at school will ensure we get a good job. We'll earn enough for a nice lifestyle and a pension when we retire.

Our conditioning, then, is all about being best equipped to find employment – to be able to compete for the best jobs. We are not taught how to turn our skills and abilities into income in other ways – how to create a business, for example, or how to become self-sufficient.

But the workplace is so different now. A good education no longer guarantees a good job or long-term security. Just look at the massed ranks of recent graduates who cannot find work. We can no longer say to our children, 'Study hard and you'll get a good job.' Traditional qualifications are no longer enough. New skills are required to survive – and thrive – in the new world of work.

That's not to say that I feel that an education is not important – quite the reverse. I think education is special for three reasons:

1. It gives us the opportunity to learn about a subject.

2. It gives us the opportunity to receive a qualification.

3. It provides us with the opportunity for personal growth which we experience as individuals studying and socializing with others – such as forming and sustaining relationships, learning to live on our own, etc. As well as the particular headline skill (e.g. bricklayer, architect, etc.), education encourages and enables us to develop a broad skill set – learning to create new concepts or ideas, develop our creativity, address issues, learn to work through tasks systematically, meet deadlines, achieve outcomes, etc.

Unfortunately we rarely recognize these core attributes in ourselves, but they are the building blocks for succeeding with Work It Out! They are never out of date. So we need to look beyond the old job titles or the names of the formal qualifications and recognize all the skills we have that will enable us to create, build and grow our workpieces.

THE OLD WORLD OF WORK

With recession, the hardship of unemployment has become a reality for many. We are encouraged to think in terms of filling in endless application forms to find a new job. But traditional job-search techniques are proving less and less effective as jobs become fewer and fewer.

Some people use the spur of unemployment to set up a business; others learn new skills. Re-skilling or re-training may make for a weightier CV, but moving from position 374 to position 178 in a league of 500 applicants is no comfort if there is only one vacancy.

HOW GOVERNMENTS USED TO CREATE JOBS

In previous recessions, governments would dust down job-creation strategies and put money into a number of measures – but how useful are these today?

- **Incentives for employers to create new jobs.** This may have been effective in the past, but now the lack of demand for products and services means employers don't have the work and can't afford to employ people, no matter how big the incentive.

- **Attracting inward investment.** In the past, tax breaks and myriad other inducements were deployed to attract international companies to set up local operations. But now, manufacturing has flown to low-cost economies and broadband networks make it possible to set up offshore services, ranging from IT to architectural design, anywhere in the world.

- **New business creation.** There are many and varied programmes that aim to provide the spark for would-be entrepreneurs. But too often this is presented as a last resort. The underlying message is not that self-employment is valued, but rather, since you can't get a job why not start a business?

- **Public sector finance** – infrastructure projects for building schools, hospitals, roads, and so on. This may be a way to maintain employment in a recession, but it is not an employment tap that can be turned on at will, especially when public finances are tight.

Beyond job-creation, there are often measures used by governments to move people off the jobless count, such as:

- **Re-training programmes** to improve an individual's ability to compete in the labour market, and/or to provide skills that are in short supply

- **Job-creation/social employment schemes** for the long-term unemployed.

But the world has moved on since the last recession, and these old methods of creating jobs are no longer suited to the task. Globalization, the Internet and changing work patterns have remade the job-creation landscape. A new approach is needed to address and take advantage of this new reality.

There are fewer jobs and the competition is greater than before. Global markets mean that everything is interconnected. Demand has fallen worldwide, and companies can't expand if there is no market for their products and services. There is far greater competition to fill any vacancies, and wages are falling. Skills-training was formerly seen as one way to make candidates more attractive to employers, but what will we re-train people for now?

The external market has little to offer the individual in the traditional job sense. And it is no longer possible to rely on governments to guarantee meaningful long-term work. Politicians have as little idea as the rest of us where the economy is going, and coherent strategies to create jobs in the short term will not be forthcoming, for some of the reasons outlined above.

So what do we do? People cannot sit back and wait two or three years for the economic cycle to turn up and hope that employment grows, too. Remember, there was initially a 'jobless recovery' after the last recession. We need to create alternative work options, for everyone in society.

THE RELUCTANT ENTREPRENEUR

What is the message going out to those who cannot find a job? In truth, there are very few palatable alternatives to being in employment. One is to start a business – but it's only a small percentage that see themselves doing this. In any case, there is little encouragement to those willing to take the risk. There's also the thought, as mentioned, that this is a bit of a last resort. It's seen as a thing to do in desperation, if you can't get 'a proper job'.

From the fruitless search for a job to the half-hearted idea for a new business that gets nowhere, it's no wonder that many lose their momentum and end up checking out daytime television and being forced to rely on benefits. Whatever the rhetoric about 'benefits scroungers', this is truly a situation few want to be in.

Despite, or maybe because of, the best efforts of television shows such as *The Apprentice* and *Dragons' Den*, entrepreneurship retains its 'wide boy', 'used car salesman' or 'Del boy' reputation. Working from home, or for yourself, should be the ultimate perk, but homeworking is frequently seen as not a 'real' job. How can you have a proper job if you don't have an employer, and what is it exactly that you do all day?

So, entrepreneurship has a negative image, and going it alone is usually seen as a second choice to mainstream employment.

Of course, there are some positive role models, people like James Dyson, Richard Branson or Stelios Haji-Ioannou, with the dynamism, the great ideas and the build-an-empire mentality to succeed. We desperately need to recognize the achievements of these individuals. But for the vast majority of us, the scale of their achievements is itself daunting. Rather than yearning to be corporate moguls, most of us merely want a solid income and an opportunity to do something useful with our lives. And, given that work takes up at least 37 hours of our week, wouldn't it be great to do work we believe in, which helps others, is fun and feels as if it's worth getting out of bed for?

JOBS AND WORK ARE NOT THE SAME THING

Job-seeking is among the many facets of modern life that have been transformed by the Internet. On the one hand, this is empowering. Rather than looking for adverts in the local paper, it is possible to browse hundreds of recruitment websites, send off CVs on spec to companies we think we would like to work for, and list our credentials in the hope of making a connection or an impression on an employer.

The problem is that all of this is *passive*. Sending out a CV involves no more than a few keystrokes on the computer. Doing a job-search via the Internet fills up time and makes us feel we are doing something useful, but it takes an increasingly heavy toll. When there are so few jobs around, the ability to be busy sending off CVs by email or filling in online forms for job websites can easily lead to increased frustration and lowered self-esteem when we get little feedback. It makes it harder to resist the corrosive thought, 'If I were any good I would have got a job by now.' And it is easy to slip into the self-blame game: 'I'm not good enough' or 'I'm a loser.'

Losing a job means that the professional and personal connections you've built up over years of being employed are suddenly taken away at the time when you need them most. The unemployed are isolated from their major support system. Not only have the ground rules changed but so too have the external environment and a major part of your personal support network. This adds to the strains and pressures brought on by unemployment.

Those facing up to the bleak reality of being unemployed need a new network to provide the positive influences that are required to rebuild confidence and show there are viable options and ways forward, easing the migration from the world of full-time employment to that of *work*.

The paradox here is that, while *jobs* may be scarce, there remains an abundance of *work*. Once we can appreciate this insight, all we need is help and advice to identify and gather the workpieces that complement and enhance our individual competencies and experience.

AFRICA AND THE ECONOMIC LADDER

In his book *The End of Poverty: How we can make it happen in our lifetime*, the renowned Harvard Economics professor and campaigner against extreme poverty, Jeffrey Sachs, explains the wealth-creation model for families in dire poverty in Africa. These families don't look for jobs. They look for ways to get food or earn money. A few hens or a couple of goats provides food for the family, and gives them eggs or milk to barter. These are the first rungs of the economic ladder. Families tend their meagre assets (hens and goats) and look for opportunities to build on them, swapping goods and exchanging skills and knowledge with others, creating additional ways to build income. This may involve getting together to make clothes, crafts or foodstuffs. This might then become a community enterprise or a business that is capable of providing skills-training for others, thus promoting and encouraging self-sufficiency and building wealth in poor communities.

BEYOND THE INDUSTRIAL REVOLUTION

The Faustian pact of the Industrial Revolution saw people move from making a living on the land, where they were in control of their own resources, to being paid more money but losing control to their new employers.

An intimate relationship with the land and nature, and the struggle to survive in often very difficult circumstances, was replaced with a relationship with an employer in a mill or factory. The search for income sources and trading opportunities was replaced by a wage for producing so much, or for working 12-hour shifts.

This also heralded the move from the world of the artisan or craftsman, whose livelihood depended on the quality and range of his or her skills, to the era of mass production, a prime objective of which was to eliminate the need for individual skills.

The centuries-long struggle to build one's own economic ladder was replaced by the factory system, which provided work for the many. There was no need to search for pieces of work; it now came packaged as a job, complete with an employer.

The sole remaining vestige of those decades of scavenging for survival in the fields of yesteryear has become the sanitized and one-dimensional approach to creating wealth known as *entrepreneurship*.

JOBS VS EMPLOYMENT – THE ALL-OR-NOTHING APPROACH

Now we have a society where the skills of individual wealth-creation are long gone. We have much to learn from Africa. In our post-industrial age where there are no longer any jobs for life, and where the option of moving from one full-time job to another is increasingly constrained, these skills are needed once more. But, as yet, efforts to rebuild such skills are at the margins. As mentioned, self-employment is often seen as a last resort, and if we are unemployed and manage to find a small piece of work around which to start building our economic ladder, we are penalized financially: benefits are withdrawn or reduced – sending out a clear message that this kind of individual effort is *not* to be encouraged.

This is wrong. Having a job has become the be-all and end-all. If you are claiming unemployment benefits it is necessary to demonstrate that you are applying for jobs and are available for work at all times. This is, however, an outdated model that was engendered and is kept alive by the traditional antipathy towards 'dole cheats'.

FINDING THE WORK YOU DREAM OF

This is not to condone fraudulent benefit claims. But clearly, a new approach is needed for supporting people whilst they establish a number of income streams that will, in the end provide long-term security. The social security system should enable people to be in control of their lives, to face down the disempowerment unleashed by being unemployed. It takes time to find the kind of work that is of real interest, is rewarding, brings with it a better work–life balance and offers security for the future.

The Work It Out! approach addresses these issues, challenges and opportunities. It is relevant to the unemployed, to those approaching retirement – and, most of all, to those in work.

But surely the employed are the safe, lucky ones? Not really. Those who are unemployed or approaching an impecunious retirement have the spur they need to do something. They need income and are keen to learn and begin the process of building a future in which they have control. As a result, they will give every good idea due consideration.

Those currently in 'secure' employment will face a very different world when they leave, or lose their job. Work now has a new context, and our understanding of what that means is unfolding. At one end of the scale, a completely different way of financing retirement is emerging. At the other end of the scale, the Internet is transforming education and skills, leaving our schools struggling to catch up.

This book is the starting point and template for approaching, understanding and thinking about this new world of work. It will act as a primer for creating the sort of life you want, showing you how to generate the income, build the resources and make the friendships you need to sustain and support you.

It is far removed from the economic model of selling your time to an employer in return for short-term income security. You will find new ways to look at things that you have taken for granted. You will gain an understanding of how to unravel your dependence on the traditional employee–employer relationship.

Taking greater responsibility for our own future is daunting, and requires us to learn new skills. The changes also call on us to help those who are less able, and to reaffirm the right to work, contribute and be rewarded and recognized for doing so.

TOP 12 REASONS FOR USING WORK IT OUT!

1. I need to make some money.

2. I'm out of work and need to rebuild my career.

3. I'm in a rut.

4. I want to spend more time with my family.

5. I'm not really happy in my current job.

6. I want to give something back.

7. I'm looking for a fresh challenge.

8. I want to have more control over my life.

9. I want to sort out my life and have a clear direction.

10. I want to enjoy getting up in the morning.

11. I want a healthier work–life balance.

12. I want a real alternative to the rat race.

The world of work is being transformed. It isn't 'full-time job' – it's Work It Out! Make it work for you.

CHAPTER 2

The Work It Out! Philosophy

The rapid rise in unemployment following a decade of job-creation and full employment provides the impetus to reshape the world of work. In some sectors Work It Out! is here already, providing exemplars for how to create and manage individual pieces of work – paid and voluntary – to create a seamless whole.

THE EVOLUTION OF WORK IT OUT!

In the old model of full employment, work is equated with financial reward. But as we all know, work is not just about getting paid. Nor is work merely about selling our time. Looking after our children, tidying the house, caring for elderly relatives and volunteering are all part of 'working' for many of us.

Work can, therefore, be defined as the *sum* of all these activities and, in the context of Work It Out!, the way we spend our time is a very important issue.

While the current recession can be seen as the tipping-point for the model of full-time, secure employment, there have been recessions before, as well as proposed solutions. One of the most obvious was the notion of 'portfolio work' as described by management guru Charles Handy in his book, *The Empty Raincoat: Making Sense of the Future*.

The Internet makes it possible for people to sell their goods and services worldwide. It also provides a ready-made infrastructure for many types of business. The growth of the online auction site eBay is a key example here. We can now reach niche markets anywhere in the world, to sell almost anything. It may at first seem unlikely, but not only is there someone out there who will cherish your unwanted bric-a-brac, there are in auction sites like eBay low-cost, accessible channels for locating them. eBay and similar sites form a critical workpiece in the income-generating 'big picture'.

Local employers and markets are still important, but they are no longer the only possibilities. You can build your own future, mixing elements drawn from the global Internet-connected community with more traditional activities, to put together your own collection of workpieces. The Work It Out! approach helps you to develop the skills, techniques and support structures you need to make the most of the incredible opportunities available, including those presented by the Internet.

This requires a radical shift in our thinking about work and jobs. A new flexibility and openness are required, accompanied by a much stronger sense of control over the way in which we generate income. Whereas before we could passively supply the skills and rely on an employer to look after us, now creating the future is our individual responsibility.

Society is at a similar juncture to that of the Industrial Revolution: technology is once again rewriting the rules of work. But while technology provides the tools for taking individual responsibility and generating our own income, as ever, the politicians are lagging behind.

Of course, some traditional jobs will remain. Charles Handy sets out a useful model in *The Empty*

Raincoat, when he describes the (theoretical) Shamrock Organization – a model for future corporate structures which, as its name suggests, is made up of three 'leaves': a core group of permanent professional employees, a cadre of part-time or temporary workers, and an army of freelancers. But in terms of the numbers of people employed in these core roles, it is useful to look back to the Industrial Revolution and recall that agricultural employment fell from over 90 per cent of the workforce to less than 5 per cent. A similar shift is about to occur as broadband Internet becomes ubiquitous.

We as individuals can access the global community, interact with colleagues across the world, buy and sell products and services to almost anyone, anywhere. As for the steam engine before it, the Internet provides the motive power for the new world of work. And Work It Out! provides the guidebook for capitalizing on the power of the Internet.

THE WORK IT OUT! APPROACH

In this new world of work, few of us will be tied to the traditional 37½-hour week. Embracing the Work It Out! method means learning to build and manage your unique collection of workpieces to provide a regular income, longer-term security and greater work satisfaction. Nor are workpieces just those elements of work we earn money from, but include voluntary work, social activities, time with our loved ones, hobbies, projects, etc.

Most people sell their time to an employer for a fixed amount. The rest of the week is spent recovering and doing domestic chores and other activities essential to modern life. From this perspective it is easy to see how paid work has come to be viewed as our 'productive' (earning) time and other activities to be seen as 'non-productive'. This undoubtedly contributed to sexual inequality: a man going out to work was a 'breadwinner' and a woman staying at home to care for children was the economically inactive 'housewife'. In turn, this paved the way for the skills of women and the activity of raising children to be devalued.

With Work It Out!, *all* time has a value – be it time that is paid for, time spent with others, time devoted to personal development, etc. Yes, we do need money, but other activities have intrinsic value as well.

A NEW VIEW OF LIFE: THE WORK IT OUT! PERSPECTIVE

- Work It Out! is about the *whole of our lives* – not just work. It provides the framework for understanding what is important to us, what can make us happy, and for realizing our ambitions. Work It Out! *encourages new thinking and creativity about work,* removing the one-dimensional, traditional view of employment. Rather than thinking solely in terms of applying for one full-time job, for example, we can start to make the transition to selecting and pulling together smaller workpieces that suit us.

- Work It Out! provides the assurance that the route to financial security can be made up of small steps and not necessarily one big leap. Given this assurance, it then becomes easier to take those small steps. Work It Out! defines the skills and approaches we need to become proactive and effective at finding workpieces – rather than being passive and waiting for vacancies to be advertised.

- Work It Out! reminds us that every workpiece we source or create, no matter how small, is a success. Because each workpiece is a step in building income, increasing control for the future. Work It Out! is a continuous process, not an 'all or nothing' gamble. Workpieces can be added or removed as your situation or needs change.

- Work It Out! puts you in control of your life and income. You no longer have to wait around for employers to decide what they want from you; you have the opportunity, today, to get started on your first workpiece.

- Work It Out! is a lifelong process. Not only are we creating and building workpieces to pay our way now, but we can be thinking of longer-term 'passive' income and scenarios in which workpieces can support us when we are older. Along with the world of work, the cosy world of an independent retirement is also dissolving and it is already the case that the State cannot meet all the needs of our growing elderly population. Work It Out! is a flexible, dynamic process that responds to our needs as our life circumstances change.

- Work It Out! enables us to build our own capital. We are investing in self-development, applying the experience gained in one workpiece to acquiring and completing new workpieces. It is no longer necessary to wait until we leave a job to apply what we know to a new task. Work It Out! is dynamic rather than linear.

- Work It Out! means that not all of our eggs are in one basket. That dreaded thought, 'What would happen if I lost my job tomorrow?' no longer causes panic. Now we not only have other workpieces, but more importantly we have the skills, experience and contacts to create new workpieces any time we like, to replace any that no longer suit. Indeed, this continuous rotation of workpieces within Work It Out! is the norm – because our situation is changing all the time.

- Work It Out! reminds us that every hour has its own value. In the old world of one job, many people got paid the same amount for each hour they worked.

Our lives were seen as split between work and home, and work was often seen solely as a means to an end. In Work It Out!, however, each hour has a different value. Looking after children, caring for a sick parent or doing voluntary work may not pay an hourly rate but these ways of spending our time are an important part of who we are. Similarly, workpieces – be they in sales, business projects or a part-time job, may all earn us different amounts.

- Work It Out! isn't just about work. The challenge is to balance our workpieces to meet all of our needs – financial, familial, social, personal and spiritual. Work It Out! and workpieces are a true reflection of us, whereas a full-time job is more a reflection of the business. Work It Out! encourages us to make productive use of all our time. It is about taking a balanced approach to all our needs, and devoting the appropriate time and effort to each one. Workpieces are about focused action.

- Work It Out! is about self-sustainability. It enables us to generate an income while having greater freedom over how we use our time and make provision for our pension and retirement needs. Work It Out! encourages personal accountability and responsibility. Each of us is empowered to make things happen and shape our own circumstances. It is the opposite of being dependent upon an employer for a job, or the State for benefits.

- Work It Out! is based on values of sharing and caring. Work It Out! provides a route to working in partnership with others. Work It Out! brings out the best of who you are. You can choose what you do, rather than being told what to do. Furthermore, Work It Out! is fully inclusive and free to everyone.

BUILDING YOUR FUTURE WITH WORK IT OUT!

As mentioned, elements of Work It Out! already exist on an informal level. What is needed now is:

- to acknowledge there is a new world of work and recognize the legitimacy of the Work It Out! approach

- to encourage our education system to develop in children and young people the core skills and competencies to take responsibility for their own work needs, to become self-sufficient and be in control of their working and personal lives

- to support each other, with practical solutions, ideas and encouragement, in developing and building workpieces.

Happiness and success are linked to a whole range of factors: work and money, a feeling of self-worth, the knowledge that we are doing something useful with our lives, our relationships with others. An important aspect of Work It Out! is to accept that you won't achieve everything overnight. This is why it is good to imagine your future life and then gently work *backwards* to the workpieces that need to be put in place to make this imagined future a reality. That beautiful house in the country, that £1,000 raised for charity, that language you've always wanted to master, that part-time job you can't wait to get to of a morning – all of these, and more, can be achieved if you are clear about the workpieces that you need to develop to make them reality.

What workpieces make up your future? Are you looking to earn a certain income every week? Have *X* amount of money in the bank? Generate income without work, such as through compound interest or some kind of investment income?

GETTING STARTED

In another of his many books, *The Age of Unreason: New Thinking for a New World*, Charles Handy talks about a 'work portfolio' as being, 'a way of describing how different bits of work in our life fit together to form a balanced whole'.

Take a moment now to imagine three or four activities that would start to give you the financial future you really want. Let's give each of these a name, for example freelancing, eBay, new business idea, etc. These are your first workpieces.

What do they look like? What will each of these look like when you are successful – that is, when they are generating an income of X per month?

1. ....

2. ....

3. ....

4. ....

How can you start to create the workpieces that you need? What are you initial thoughts? Can you start to imagine how these workpieces could develop from now to become real? Can you see how your idea or area of interest could become a specific service, product or income stream?

To start, do you need to do some research on Google – to see what already exists on this topic? to find out what other providers are offering and charging? to see how others are marketing and selling this service?

Another example of a first step might be to send a letter or email to some potential customers to ask about your idea or service, see what they currently have in place and what issues or needs they have.

So, what is the first thing you need to do to get each one of your workpieces moving?

....

Which is your priority piece? Start now! Which workpiece will you move forward today? Write down what you will do to move this forward *today*.

....

I was fortunate enough to meet Charles Handy at his home during the last recession. At that time I was running a training and employment business, helping people back into work. We were finding jobs for 5,000 people and helping 4,000 to get new qualifications every year. Charles and I had a wonderful discussion about how the portfolio idea would become reality. He found some of the employment experiments my business had trialled, such as enterprise factories and the programmes we ran in Romania and Albania (two countries which were then encountering unemployment for the first time), particularly interesting. For him these examples offered possible clues into how the world of work might evolve in the future.

As Handy puts it, '... Retirement, unemployment and redundancy only make sense in job-work terms. The optimist's scenario sees work and leisure and adequate money for all, with lots of room for individual variation ...'

Handy's vision of the work portfolio has taken root and evolved in a range of ways. Work It Out! is, at heart, about who we are as humans – integrating the way, the time and the place in which we create workpieces in our daily lives. In the Internet age the old work–life split has disappeared. Computers, phones, email and texting keep us in constant contact with what is happening in all aspects of our lives – no matter where we are or what time it is.

It is of little use, then, to talk of work–life balance. We need to manage all of our workpieces effectively as part of our overall needs and aims. Many complain about information overload, about 24/7 communications, about the need to respond across time zones. Work It Out! seeks to utilize this connectedness in a positive way and apply it to balancing out all aspects of our lives – income, family, hobbies, projects, and so on.

WHERE DO YOU WORK?

The location of work has expanded from the four walls of the office or factory to take in any location with a wireless signal, and of course the home. There are no longer any clear dividing lines between what we used to call work and leisure. The way that we manage this is dependent on the workpiece we are engaged with, rather than our physical location. This has effectively shifted control to us – which is great if we know how to create new workpieces.

We now move effortlessly between the mobile phone and computers, in the office, on the train or at home. We can get on with other activities and manage our work tasks at the same time, seamlessly progressing from ordering groceries and booking tickets online to researching a new project, whilst completing another. Tea breaks are taken at the computer and don't involve a 'break' at all. The Internet enables us to 'work', 'chat' and 'play' all at the same time, at any time. We no longer 'clock-in' or work only at the office.

The idea of building a portfolio job around different pieces of work is often presented as an option open only to seasoned business professionals with years of experience in different walks of life, roles and positions, who can step effortlessly into this consultancy or that non-executive directorship. The opposite is true. Work It Out! is for everyone – irrespective of their life situation, background or experience.

Work It Out! has a philosophy of shared success. Unlike many business models which are competitive, solitary in operation and exclusive to one particular social group, Work It Out! welcomes all comers.

CASE STUDY: THE MARKETING SPECIALIST

My mobile rang first thing this morning. It was a call from a Senior Marketing Manager called Richard about the opportunities he had just learned about of working as a consultant with one of our businesses. He was experienced at board level, confident in his ability and said he had good interpersonal skills.

His first questions were about money and earnings. He then went on to ask what services he would be delivering and to whom.

I slowed him down a little and pointed out that all this information is on our website: we provide support to individuals who have lost their jobs, companies making people redundant, Local Authorities that want to provide practical support to the jobless in their communities and Government departments looking to support policies that actively promote the new world of work.

'Do you have experience in any of these areas?' I asked. 'Yes, I've been made redundant and have been applying for jobs for three months now,' was the response. He went on to give the familiar tale of sending out countless CVs and no one responding – never mind offering him an interview.

I posed the question, 'If you have been doing something for so long that hasn't worked, why keep on doing it? If we keep getting no response then surely it's time to change our behaviour?' He couldn't see it. He was brilliantly qualified, had marvellous experience and was confident – and yet was getting absolutely nowhere. It couldn't be his fault.

I gently posed the question another way: 'What if a major commercial client hired you as a Marketing Director because their current campaigns were not working? Would the client just keep spending time and money running the same campaigns?' The penny was beginning to drop – albeit slowly.

Richard knew he was stuck in the job application-despondency trap. The problem is we know no real alternative to the crazy CV, letter and email-bombardment approach to finding work. And now countless job sites are creating even more places to send CVs. Social networking sites allow us to contact lots of friends and colleagues, but what is the message we are sending out? This is where Richard was stuck.

Of course he isn't alone. We have all been taught that this is the way to build a career: acquire skills, get a job, get a better job, retire. Job done, so to speak. The new world of work isn't like this. All of us have to dismantle what we know about getting work and learn a new approach. The good news for Richard is that all of his skills remain highly relevant, if he can appreciate how to deploy them in a different way.

'Are you talking about self-employment?' he asked, evidently hoping I wasn't. But the label 'self-employment' – or indeed, 'employment', 'entrepreneurship', 'part-time work' – no longer apply. All these old definitions are no longer helpful, nor indeed valid. One analogy is to consider the status of banks a couple of years ago and look at them now. How did you view them then and how do you rate them now? It's a totally different ball game.

In My Slippers

My email pings: Pradip has just invited me to one of his virtual training courses. He sits in his slippers and works with clients all over the world. They listen to him on the phone whilst he takes them through a PowerPoint training programme on their computer. They can ask him questions and form virtual groups to discuss particular points, whilst Pradip goes off and has a coffee. The groups then report back on an interactive online whiteboard which everyone in the session can see.

This virtual, Internet-mediated approach to training works well for international companies, saving on hotel bills, flights and time away from the job.

I remember my days as a trainer when I would be running to departure gates, struggling with flipcharts, delegate manuals, overhead projector, overnight bag and so on. And now Pradip is sitting – who knows where? – in his slippers.

It's the same group training process, of course, just with different technology.

We're Cooking Again

Of late, pre-prepared and packaged ready meals have been falling out of favour. Partly because in these penny-pinching times they are too expensive, partly because the incredible amount of packaging that accompanies them is seen as environmentally unfriendly and, given the liberal use of salt and other additives, their nutritional value is questioned. There has been a swing back to cooking, as exemplified by supermarket adverts in which celebrity chefs show how to cook a healthy meal for the family by throwing a few simple ingredients together.

In creating our new meals we not only change our attitude to the ready-packaged kind, we also re-learn how to put ingredients together to make different meals. We're cooking again.

Full-time jobs are to the new world of work as the pre-packaged ready meal is to home cooking. The raw ingredients of work (time, skills, experience, payment and so on) are no longer packaged as a pre-determined recipe or job. We are working with ingredients and creating new meals (our workpieces). We can follow the recipe books or create our own concoctions. The aim is to create tasty dishes that add up to a healthy, balanced diet.

We Don't Just Have to Be One Thing

So, it's no longer appropriate to think in terms of the old labels of job = employee, or self-employed = entrepreneur or training/education = student. Instead we need to be thinking in broader terms of how we create and put our Work It Out! workpieces together.

In the new world of work we can have a collection of labels.

CASE STUDY: BARRY

I was struck by this new fluidity when I encountered Barry, a college student in London. Barry works part-time in a pub, is writing his first novel, selling collectibles on eBay and teaching kids to play football on a Sunday morning.

These are Barry's Work It Out! pieces – defined by his needs for short-term income (working part-time in the pub and selling collectibles on eBay), longer-term career plans (college course), community spirit (teaching kids to play football), physical exercise (ditto) and creativity (writing a novel – which, if successful, would also put some passive income in place for the longer term).

It is such an understatement to say that Barry is just a student.

WHAT DO YOU DO?

Our old labels for each other – shop assistant, entrepreneur, factory worker or charity volunteer – do little to capture the wealth of skills, interests, capabilities and needs, either of ourselves or others.

When one job was the norm, we could pose the question 'What do you do?', expecting an answer such as secretary, cook or pilot, teacher, cleaner or barrister. Now, more appropriate questions are, 'What sorts of things do you do?' Other questions will include: How many workpieces have you got? What are your latest workpieces? I've got this great idea for a workpiece but just need someone to help me with it. Any new or exciting workpieces? What workpiece do you really want to create or build at the moment?

Similarly, it's no longer a question of, 'What [one thing] do you want to be when you grow up?' but rather 'What kinds of different things do you want to do/achieve/be when you grow up?'

CONVERSATIONS WITH A WORK IT OUT! WORKER AND A JOBSEEKER

How's the Job-search Going?

'WORK IT OUT' WORKER:
Brilliantly! I'm currently developing a whole new approach to the way I work.

JOBSEEKER:
Awful. I've had no interviews for three weeks now.

What Are You Doing?

'WORK IT OUT' WORKER:
I'm a Work It Out! worker – which means that I'm working on creating a series of workpieces, increasing my income and learning to manage my time in a much more productive way.

JOBSEEKER:
Battling on. You know what it's like.

What's Next Then?

'WORK IT OUT' WORKER:
I currently have three key workpieces that I'm concentrating on. The first two are bringing in some income and now I'm focusing on getting the third off the ground.

JOBSEEKER:
I just have to keep getting the application forms in. What else can I do, eh?

INPLOYMENT

The traditional way we have positioned ourselves in employment, either with an employer or by being self-employed (including setting up a business), changes in the much more fluid and accommodating new world of Work It Out! Instead of being either 1) employed, 2) self-employed or 3) unemployed – we need to start considering ourselves *inployed*!

This means we can do freelance work, sell things we no longer need, take part-time roles, enjoy temporary assignments, build our own brand, work on projects with others, and so on, as we move seamlessly between what we used to call employment and self-employment.

Inployment involves taking responsibility for our own income.

There are plenty of rejections waiting out there for those looking for work. It is a solitary process framed in competition with others. And when it comes to the alternative of self-employment, there are many obstacles and much to learn before we can hope to become successful.

Inployment, on the other hand, is proactive and positive. We take responsibility for creating our workpieces, and we also look for ways to help others with theirs. It's a collaborative and inclusive approach.

Those in traditional full-time employment can also enjoy the wider world of inployment as they seek to add new workpieces and derive greater value from their current role. For example, some people may prefer to work fewer hours than the normal 37½ a week. Others may see the opportunity to be more effective in their organizations by restructuring their role or responsibilities. Some may see ways to create other workpieces for themselves, or add value for their traditional employer by leveraging their experience and contacts in different ways. In other words, it is possible even for those in full employment to have other outside workpieces and move towards inployment.

And what about those who are currently unemployed? In one sense, of course, no one is ever truly unemployed – everyone has responsibilities they must fulfil, and activities that are important to them or that they enjoy: they may care for loved ones or look after the house, for example. The label 'unemployment' totally fails to recognize this, whereas in Work It Out!

inployment includes the possibility that we may be 'unwaged' but still involved in creating workpieces and moving forward. The challenge is to ensure that the pieces of work we do contribute either to a greater whole (the smooth running of a household, for instance, or the successful bringing-up of children) or to providing us with the income level we need.

Instead of being forced into one of the three categories of employment/self-employment/unemployment, we can now place ourselves on the continuum of inployment. We are all inployed in Work It Out!, just at different points along the continuum. We are all striving to improve our situation and keen to work with others to help them and us succeed.

INSIDE THE JIGSAW BOX

Take a look at the cover of the box a jigsaw puzzle comes in: there's the completed picture as it will be once we have completed the puzzle. With Work It Out! we take the elements that are important to us and create our own picture. These elements are likely to include our family, the place where we live, our house and car, friends and so on. The picture will also include our hopes for the future, what defines us as individuals, and our aspirations.

One of the major tasks in all of this is to be clear about where you are going and what you want to achieve. Work It Out! is not merely about collecting together disparate workpieces to earn enough money for now. It's about erecting an overall framework to guide you going forward.

The picture on the lid of your Work It Out! box is your life in the round. The workpieces that make up this picture are not all in the box yet. You have to create them. And you can be working on many of them at the same time, to make the picture that is important for you. And this picture can change as you create it, adding or subtracting workpieces. It's always a work in progress (like life!).

FORGET THE WORK–LIFE BALANCE

There are practical challenges in fitting workpieces together as we create them: How well does our latest project fit with our family life? How well does our weekend work fit with our voluntary activities?

Work It Out! doesn't talk about work–life balance. It is an outdated concept which holds that 'work' is separate from 'life'. In the modern world we know that work is an integral part of life, not separate from it. Rather than dealing with the artificial construct of work first, with life coming a poor second, Work It Out! focuses on the overall shape of the picture and the relative size and shape of each of the individual pieces. Are you spending too much time on one activity? Are you not earning enough from another activity? Have you thought about passive income sources – particularly as you get older?

Work It Out! is not simply a collection of work elements. It's about the creation, shaping, development, organizing, pulling-together and balancing of these elements. And it's not a one-off event, but a dynamic process that changes as our lives change. We leave school, we get married, we have children, someone close to us dies. Key events cause our needs to change and our workpieces to change also.

Work It Out! workpieces have a lifespan, too, and will come and go from our collection. A task may no longer be relevant to our needs, or we may find a better or more enjoyable way to generate the same income, or a different way to achieve an objective. Work It Out! is a continuous process throughout our lives. It is dynamic, flexible and responsive to our needs. We build – and build on – the skills of creating and managing our workpieces as we go through life. These skills continue to be honed and tuned as we grow and learn.

Work It Out! is not a place of uncertainty, or lack of opportunity, or fear. Quite the opposite. It is a place of opportunity, partnership, access, for living the life you believe you should. The tools are here – the Internet, networking sites, places to sell, instant communication – and a growing team of people ready to support and help you.

What you need now are the personal skills and understanding, the confidence to have a go, and the reassurance that others are with you.

CHAPTER 3

Work It Out! Workpieces

It may be possible to catch a glimpse of what a working life based on a series of projects, or workpieces, could be like. But the question is how to start putting a collection together, and how to get over the hump of needing to maintain an income stream at the same time.

There are plenty of workpieces available; you just need to be organized and disciplined to get your Work It Out! career off the ground.

WHERE DO I START?

Work It Out! is not a solitary activity. It's not a question of sitting down, looking at your computer and wondering what to do. It's not about looking in the newspapers for job adverts.

Work It Out! requires a different mindset and a different schedule of activities. It's about building different types of relationships with the specific intention of creating workpieces. You may have a project between one other person and yourself or, in a totally different initiative, four of you may get together to share the work.

The starting point of the Work It Out! process is conversation and interaction, and of beginning to identify two or three strands you want to pursue and develop. Remember: 'What do you really want to do?'

After this it's about building relationships to tease out these ideas and trying to develop them into workpieces. For example:

- Meet former work colleagues. Try and identify an area that you are interested in where you may be able to develop a product or service. Discuss this with others and try and create projects and initiatives.

- Get onto social networking sites such as LinkedIn, Twitter, Ecademy and Facebook and use your links within these networks to work with others to create workpieces.

BUT I NEED INCOME NOW!

Yes, it's hard to concentrate on future projects, initiatives and plans when you need to earn money now.

Full-time paid employment may be in short supply, but there is plenty of work out there – be it serving in a pub, window-cleaning, gardening, or selling on eBay. Most of us could find some way of earning a bit of money now if we really needed to. There are probably two things stopping us:

1. Thinking 'This type of work won't pay anywhere near the amount of money I need.'

We are used to thinking in terms of the 37½-hour-a-week job. Why should we take a job that will only give us a fraction of that?

But the choice is straightforward. We can go on hoping that someone will offer us the magic job, or we can get started creating our own future – one that we are in control of. We can be earning some income now.

Remember, we all have to start somewhere and these are only starting pieces. The first activity you undertake is not your new career. But it provides you with some income as you build the work you really want. It's a stepping stone to a better workpiece. As your time fills with more relevant and productive activity, so you can drop these 'starter activities'. So look to your future, not the past.

2. Ego: 'Why should someone of my skills and experience be "reduced" to this type of work?' 'What will the neighbours say?'

Work It Out! is about helping you to get onto your economic ladder and start climbing fast. It's no use standing at the bottom looking up at the top and thinking about the neighbours (who may, in any case, be in a similar situation). You're never going to get to that top rung with one jump – so make up your mind to start climbing now.

In the new world of work, activity is essential. Doing things that help to create workpieces is essential. Every hour is crucial. You simply can't afford to slip back into the old routine of sitting down to watch afternoon TV after you've checked the papers for jobs or sent off an application or two.

It's all about productivity – working on all of your workpieces at the same time – pushing each one forward every day until it becomes a reality, turning initial activities into greater income and more rewarding roles, and learning to take control of every single hour as you build the life that you want.

THERE ARE LOADS OF WORKPIECES TO CHOOSE FROM

Let us briefly mention the top 20 workpiece categories that have emerged from Work It Out! workshops and networking. Read through this list carefully, considering each workpiece in turn:

- freelance workpieces

- selling online workpieces

- relationship workpieces

- writing workpieces

- making things workpieces

- holiday workpieces

- charity workpieces

- part-time workpieces

- hobby workpieces

- family workpieces

- creative workpieces

- spiritual workpieces

- caring workpieces

- temporary job workpieces

- personal development workpieces

- community workpieces

- professional association workpieces

- health and wellbeing workpieces

- bartering workpieces

- e-learning workpieces.

Not all workpieces have to be turned into money. It's all about balance. Read through the list of 20 workpiece categories again and see if you can identify just one possible idea for making each one work for you.

COLLECT YOUR WORKPIECES AND GET ORGANIZED

It's essential to get your workpieces organized so that you can easily manage all that is happening. The important points here are:

1. You need a means of visualizing the range of workpieces you are spending your time on, now. Some people use a spreadsheet, some their phone, others a Work It Out! notebook and or a diagram on the wall.

2. You need to look at this every day to remind yourself about your aims, your priorities and what you need to do today for each workpiece.

3. You need to keep your chart, diagram or notes up to date. Everything you do to move one of your workpieces forward is a success, so make a note of it – and congratulate yourself.

WOULD YOU WORK FOR NOTHING?

CASE STUDY: ALEX

I was speaking to Alex, a former CEO of a US company based in Ireland. He had just been made redundant in his late forties. Realizing that his chances of finding suitable rewarding employment were very low, he choose to invest in himself for three months.

In this time one of the things Alex did was to find a small business network which operated locally. He checked out how it worked and was funded, and what sort of businesses the members were involved with. After talking to the organizers he went along to a couple of meetings and then offered to deliver a couple of free training sessions on areas of interest to the network. As an accountant he had lots of good advice on cashflow, credit control and cost management, which were all identified as priority areas.

After giving two talks he had his first two clients, one engaging him for one day a week and the other for two days per month. He had his first two workpieces and the start of a new Work It Out! career.

This same approach can work for personnel specialists, marketing managers, IT experts and a number of other professionals. Working for free gives you the ultimate competitive advantage. Do it with a genuine desire to add value and help other businesses. In the end they will be buying your personal skills and helpful attitude, as much as your technical ability.

Make it clear that you are seeking to work on a small number of projects. Put a value on what you do so that people realize the value of your expertise.

- Work for free.

- Try and add value.

- Make it easy for others to engage you in some capacity.

- Put a value on what you do.

Whom could you help? Is there a small business network in your area? What kinds of organizations are likely to benefit from your skills and experience?

APPLY – EVEN FOR THE EASY WORK

Hunting down that one elusive job may succeed for some, but unfortunately not for most of us in these difficult economic times. Everyone knows that when that elusive vacancy comes up, the competition will be intense. You may strike lucky and succeed early on. If not, you are likely to be on a slippery slope of declining confidence, plummeting motivation and increasing stress. And the longer you are out of work, the more an employer is likely to ask, 'I wonder why they've been out of work for so long?' The job-hunting model stacks the odds against you. Don't fall into the despondency trap.

Each job application or CV you send is filled with hope. There's a sense of achievement as you drop the envelope into the postbox or click 'Send'. But this is the point at which things are now out of your control. From now on, someone else is making the decisions about you. Repeated rejections turn any sense of hope into hopelessness: 'There's no point – I got three rejections this week and six didn't even bother to answer.'

Job-hunting can be a disempowering process – unless we are in control and not totally dependent upon getting that one big job. When we look for part-time or temporary jobs, however, or a short-term assignment to add to other income activities as part of our Work It Out! plan, we have a much greater chance of success – and a lot of the pressure is off and we can be more relaxed about the process.

YOUR STARTER WORKPIECES

By creating your own workpieces, you remain the one in control. You are out there gathering pieces of work – adding a task here or a couple of hours there – building up your commitment. It's positive. You are meeting people, going places, doing a variety of activities – and engaged in a wide range of ideas and opportunities. Some things you try may not work – or may even fall into the 'crazy ideas' category. But this is all part of the creative process. Work It Out! is not about instant perfection. It's about creating and building workpieces that move you closer to where you want to be in life.

Starter workpieces can be stepping stones to the workpiece you really want to create.

Part-time or temporary/seasonal work contracts are the easier jobs to get. Don't worry about your ego or fret about the hourly rate at this stage. The key question is, can it bring you income now? Can it be your first or a new starter workpiece? Treat this as important training and remember you are being paid while you are learning to build your workpieces. Every piece you add is a success. You can swap and change workpieces later when you have too many.

Think of an easy starter workpiece that could get you moving in the right direction *right now*. This could just be the key to unlocking your future ...

ANSWER ....

INDIVIDUALS IN TOUGH SITUATIONS

The homeless, those with disabilities or long-term illness, or in situations where they are devoting their lives to caring or other family responsibilities, are clearly at an economic disadvantage. They are often left out or marginalized.

Work It Out! aims to bring everyone into the mainstream and to provide practical support to all. This is not a 'charitable' activity, rather it is at the core of the Work It Out! ethos: to be supportive and helpful to all those we work with. It reflects the fact that Work It Out! is about everyone being successful.

A word of advice or encouragement, an idea or suggestion, some assistance with graphics, editorial or software, can have a major impact on the creation of new workpieces.

CASE STUDY: ROGER

At the age of 61 Roger Wilson-Hinds set out to develop Screenreader, a technology for people who are blind or visually impaired, in which the computer reads aloud what is displayed on the monitor. Over 100,000 people all over the world have accessed the software for free.

We may not all have the skill to do something like this, which can make a big difference to a large number of people. But we could all, for example, contribute to provide respite care for someone who is a full-time carer.

Workpieces are the way that we spend all of our 'non-maintenance' time – our 'maintenance' time is the time we spend sleeping, eating and attending to our personal care (bathing, dressing, cleaning our teeth, etc.).

Workpieces are not a second-class substitute for having a 'proper' job.

We are all in a position to help others create workpieces – by asking questions or offering encouragement, suggestions and our time. Everyone can be a workpiece motivator.

Create an environment that fosters workpiece development. Encourage and support links that fertilize the creation of new workpieces, and celebrate successes.

THE SIX WORKPIECE LAWS

1. Your current workpieces are stepping stones to better workpieces. Don't get stuck thinking that a particular workpiece is the be-all and end-all of your existence.

2. Workpieces are created by you. They grow, evolve and then reach a natural endpoint or are discarded. This is the natural order of the new world of work. Don't expect your workpieces to last forever, or never to change as you progress them. Always be on the lookout for ways to create add-ons or generate new opportunities – from each workpiece.

3. Workpieces will only materialize when you act. While other people can provide ideas, advice and help, only you can create a workpiece. You have to say, 'I'm going to do this' or 'I'm going to try to...'

4. Every workpiece is unique. Each one is based on your needs at that moment and the opportunity you created. This is important because, as you become more proficient at developing the workpieces you want, this uniqueness adds to your identity and to your individual brand. Yes – you can be a brand (if you want to be), just waiting to be made manifest by a workpiece.

5. Never underestimate any workpiece. It is only a starting point. Who knows what the customers you meet might say to you, what new relationships you will build, or what further ideas it will spark? So put 100 per cent effort into every workpiece. As my Dad says, 'If it's worth doing, it's worth doing well.'

6. You should never be snide about another person's efforts or workpieces. If you doubt its commercial

impact or potential, offer some practical support and help make it a success. In other words, be part of the solution.

What Makes a Successful Workpiece?

- There is a positive outcome for you. The workpiece generates income, is something you enjoy, reflects a part of you, enables you to contribute or help others. *It meets your needs*.

- It makes the world a better place in some small way – cleaner, tidier, safer, kinder, more compassionate, healthier, happier, more secure. A successful workpiece has the potential to reach out beyond the initial need to generate money.

- A successful workpiece enables you to grow as a person, increases your level of fulfilment and allows you to move forward.

WORK IT OUT! AND SUBCONTRACTING

Work It Out! is very different from the kind of subcontracting via websites which allow individual users to tender for bits of work. While work found by this route could be an element of Work It Out!, it is important not to limit your focus to subcontracting, which carries the risk of you becoming too dependent on one income source, or indeed one website.

In addition, Work It Out! is fundamentally more proactive. It's not just about responding to what others need, it is about creating workpieces that are inspired by your own interests, needs and ambitions.

Rather than simply repeating similar work, or providing similar services through freelancing or subcontracting, Work It Out! adds the crucial dimension of allowing you to experiment and reach out to others with similar interests or complementary skills, to try something new and different.

Work It Out! is not limited to finding another means to carrying on getting paid for doing the same things as before. What you end up doing rests on your enthusiasm and determination to make something happen.

YOUR IDEAL WORK IT OUT! PICTURE

Now stand back and visualize your ideal Work It Out! picture. Can you imagine two or three different income streams? Can you see how you might gradually build on these? How many workpieces would you like? Which workpieces will you get up and running quickly? Who can help you? What will you be doing three months from now? How will your picture be shaping up?

Don't worry if the final picture is unclear. Work It Out! is a process, and opportunities and ideas will emerge as you engage in the process. Your brain will develop a new way of thinking – one where it can freely create ideas – rather than waiting for the post and another dreaded rejection letter. Keep asking yourself, 'How many workpieces would I like?', 'Who can help me?' and 'What will I be doing in three months' time?' – and the other questions in the paragraph above – and stay on track.

If something happens to set you back a few days, where you get nothing done, don't worry. This is a cumulative process, so just pick up your planner and keep all the pieces moving forward.

Life cannot be totally planned or mapped out. Problems arise, people get ill, unexpected crises happen, circumstances change. That's life. Accept this and review your plan accordingly.

Work It Out! Colleagues

Now that you're thinking about Work It Out! and how it might help you, why not discuss the idea with a colleague, family member or online friend?

---

12 POPULAR WORKPIECES

Hard work brings its own rewards. Here are 12 possible workpieces on which to focus your initial efforts. Please do feel free to add some ideas of your own!:

1. Part-time, temporary or seasonal work of any kind

2. Selling your time to others on an *ad hoc* basis

3. Doing voluntary work (for example, helping young people at evenings/weekends with sport activities in a supervising, coaching or transport role, or helping to set up a drama group, organize a charity concert or fashion show, or setting up a business or investment club, etc.)

4. Using assets to generate cash (for example, selling on eBay or at car boot sales)

5. Caring for a family member (or carer)

6. Writing and selling e-books

7. Making, growing and adding value to products. Adding value means you can get paid more for your product by adding something. For example, you can add value to bedding plants by putting them in a colourful little bucket. Why not add a bow for Mother's Day? You can add value to home-made

jam with a label that says 'Mrs Whitton's traditional home-made farmhouse jams'. Why not wrap the jar in cellophane to make it even more special?

8. Linking up with colleagues to see how together you can use your combined skills to create income from your joint expertise

9. Swapping your skills with someone else to create a product/service

10. Showing others how to perform particular tasks

11. Researching a perceived need as part of a possible project

12. Creating a new product/venture with others

THINGS TO REMEMBER

1. We all have to learn to be more proactive about our income, no longer assuming the right job is out there waiting for us. In the new world of work we have to create our own future.

2. This is *fun*. It recognizes our many talents, skills and interests and encourages us to cultivate and pursue them. We no longer have to devote our lives to a job we hate.

3. By exploring new possibilities we can fulfil our potential in all our areas of interest.

4. It will take time and determination to succeed, but we are the only ones that can make it happen. We can get training and support from others, but we have to get out there and create or find the pieces.

5. Managing workpieces is a challenge. Making sure that workpieces are complementary and fit well together is a new skill that will take time to master.

CASE STUDY: ADRIAN

I went to collect a couple of pictures from the picture-framing shop, which is owned and managed by a quiet young man called Adrian. He has built up a good local business, and I was interested to hear of his initiative in selling prints online. But it was when I asked him what he was doing for his holidays this year that Adrian surprised me. 'I'm off to Venice for a seven-day course on trading future options. It's the advanced one. I did the basic course last year.'

I didn't expect *that* response! But I should have: Adrian has one successful workpiece up and running, and this was allowing him to develop another income stream and another workpiece.

WORKPIECE IDEAS YOU CAN START WITH TODAY

Here is a set of creative questions to help you explore possibilities for your starter workpieces. Don't fall into the trap of only doing what you have always done. Think about what you would *really like to do*, and then see if any of these suggestions can help you to move in that direction.

What Items Could You Grow or Make, then Sell?

This is often referred to as 'homeworking' or 'cottage industry'. These can be craft items, eco-friendly cards, organic foodstuffs, knitted goods, scented candles.

1. ....

2. ....

3. ....

What Book, Guide or Manual Could You Write and Sell?

Publishing is now instantaneous. We type the copy, click pdf, and immediately we have a document to distribute by email to the world. PayPal makes getting payment instantaneous as well.

What might you publish? You could consider 'How to' manuals, information on your favourite hobby, travel guides, money-saving tips, and so on. What are you really interested in?

1. ....

2. ....

3. ....

What Services Could You Provide and Sell?

Here's a sample of the kinds of services for which there is likely to be a local market: Handyman, gardening, cleaning, ironing, window-cleaning, computer repair, sports coaching, computer skills, football training, personal cookery, car valeting, translation services, tutoring.

1. ....

2. ....

3. ....

In your local area you need to let people know you are there. Here are a few easy and low-cost ways to publicize your services:

- a sign/poster for noticeboards in local shops, community centres, post offices

- leaflet drops to homes/businesses

- small advert in the local paper

- web directories.

What Skills Could You Share and Sell?

What can you train others in? How about bread-making, car maintenance for beginners, dance classes, languages, web marketing, book-keeping?

1. ....

2. ....

3. ....

What Could You Sell on eBay?

Everyone can make money on eBay. Check out the site to see what others are selling and, more importantly, what people are buying and how much they are paying for it. Most of us have stuff around the house and in the garage that can be converted into cash. Car boot sales can be good places to sell things or, armed with knowledge of what is selling well on eBay, they are good places to acquire stock.

1. ....

2. ....

3. ....

How Might You Utilize Your Assets?

List one way someone could make money from their garden by growing fruit, vegetables and flowers, making jams and pickles:

....

List one way someone could make money from their car or van, for example, doing deliveries:

....

List a way someone could make money from their computer, for example, typing documents:

....

List one way that someone could make money from their spare room or empty garage, for example, providing bed and breakfast, or having a lodger:

....

Now list all your assets and possible ways of generating income from each. Remember, this is an exercise to get you thinking creatively – you don't have to like the ideas or have any intentions of putting them into practice.

1. ....
2. ....
3. ....
4. ....

Getting More Ideas for Workpieces

- Do research – stories in the press, adverts, surveys, questionnaires about your areas of interest.

- Identify gaps in the market by looking for products and services available in other areas that could be offered where you are.

- Know your local market.

- Think about marketing your skills, products or services on the web to reach a global market.

- Spot opportunities – created by location, situation, incidents, developments.

- Look for niche markets for specialized products or services.

CHAPTER 4

Creating Your Own Workpieces

Anyone who has previously been in full-time employment is used to having all their work-time activity dictated by the needs of the job. This makes it hard to generate ideas for workpieces. This chapter gives you practical advice and exercises for creating and building workpieces, pulling in fellow Work It Out! workers and finding resources on the Internet.

GENERATING IDEAS FOR
POSSIBLE WORKPIECES

Now we are going to explore possibilities and ask what-if questions to identify ways in which you can create workpieces. For example:

- What if I apply that experience in a different way?

- What if I tried that suggestion to see what happens?

- Who could I get to help me with this idea?

Instead of categorizing your skills in terms of jobs you have had, see your life as a *process* and consider all the different skills, qualifications and experiences that you have gathered along the way.

With the next three exercises, the purpose is to look at yourself and your life to date in a 'non-job' way. The aim is to deconstruct previous jobs or experiences into their key elements. The result will be to uncover a wealth of Work It Out! opportunities.

With this information to hand, you'll be able to write down all the ways to market your skills and experience as a service or a new product, to meet a need at the moment, to solve a particular problem for others, to help others to be more successful or make their lives easier.

LOOKING AT YOURSELF IN SIX NEW WAYS

1. What **skills** do I have that could help to create products or services I could offer?

What are your skills? What are you good at?	Possible services or products from this
1	1
2	2
3	3
4	4
5	5
6	6
7	7
8	8
9	9
10	10

2. What **experience** do I have that could be useful in creating new products or services?

Experiences – what have you achieved? What have been your successes? What have you learned at different stages in your life?	Possible services or products from this
1	1
2	2
3	3
4	4
5	5
6	6

3. What **qualifications** do I have that could help me to create products or services?

Qualifications – formal and informal. What could you help others to learn about?	Possible services or products from this
1	1
2	2
3	3
4	4
5	5
6	6

4. How might **things that I like to do** be turned into new products or services?

Things you like to do – at work, at home, in your spare time, etc.	Possible services or products from this
1	1
2	2
3	3
4	4
5	5
6	6

5. How can the **areas that I am really interested in** be turned into new products or services?

Areas and topics that you are really interested in ... what would you like to know more about?	Possible services or products from this
1	1
2	2
3	3
4	4
5	5
6	6

6. How can my **ambition for the future** give me ideas for new products or services?

Ambition for the future – what would you like to see happen in your life? What will you be doing five years from now?	Possible services or products from this
1	1
2	2
3	3
4	4
5	5
6	6

This next exercise is best done with a friend or colleague.

£100 BY NEXT WEEK – A WORKPIECE EXERCISE FOR TWO

If you and a friend or colleague had to generate £100 each by next week, what would you do?

Can you list 10 realistic possibilities that could help you to achieve this target? Sit down with your colleague and come up with your best ideas. Ensure each of you has a clear plan. Then go and see if you can make it happen! Keep in close contact over the course of the week and if one of you is struggling, the other should help out. This task can only be considered successful if both of you make £100.

It will be helpful to:

- Break the £100 down into pieces.

- Look for lots of ideas, not just one.

- Think about what you enjoy, what you're good at and what gives you a buzz.

1 ....

2 ....

3 ....

4 ....

5 ....

6 ....

7 ....

8 ....

9 ....

10 ....

This exercise brings us back to the reality of being able to generate modest amounts of funding at reasonably short notice.

Did you list ten ways to achieve this target?

Here are some ideas you may have thought of ...

- washing cars, cleaning windows or doing gardening

- providing an ironing service, help with cleaning, doing some babysitting

- selling £100 worth of stuff on eBay

- working in a local bar or cafe

- delivering a training course or coaching session

- providing home hairdressing for the housebound

- fixing computers

- showing others how to use Facebook and Twitter to market their services

- selling at a car boot sale or auction.

BECOME A BEST-SELLING AUTHOR IN THREE WEEKS

This exercise is to show that you are an expert, that others can benefit from your expertise, and that you can become wealthy.

Part One – What's Your Passion?

When I was 16 I read a book by Joe Karbo called *The Lazy Man's Way to Riches*. Karbo, a pioneer of self-publishing, said a couple of things that have helped me in my life. The first is that each of us knows more about something than half the world does. It may be a particular interest, an area of expertise, a skill or a particular experience.

Half the world is a pretty big market to go at. So what is it that you know about or have an interest in? What are you good at? What do you enjoy? What gives you a buzz?

Write down what you enjoy, what you know about, your passion. List at least three very different areas or topics. Be as specific as you can.

1. ....

2. ....

3. ....

Part Two – A Great Title

The second thing Karbo wrote was that you should give your information (or book) a great title. Have you noticed the titles of books at airports or train stations? *I Can Make You Thin*, *The Laws of Happiness*, *Seven Habits of Highly Successful People*, etc. That's why Karbo called his book, *The Lazy Man's Way to Riches* rather than *How to Make Money*. He sold thousands of copies of his self-published book with small ads headed, 'Most people are too busy earning a living to make any money.'

I put this into practice a number of years ago when I was building a training company in the UK. Our two most popular training courses for Human Resources staff were: 'Training – What's the financial return?' This was a course for HR people who wanted to be able to show how training contributed to profits, or put forward a stronger case for a higher training budget. This one course accounted for over 60 per cent of our open-course income.

The second most popular course was 'Liven Up Your Training' – a course to provide trainers with exercises, games, ice-breakers and so on. Many trainers wanted to be more effective or more entertaining, or to add something a bit different or special to their courses.

Now it's your turn: come up with some titles for your book(s) on the subjects you've jotted down that will encourage people to want to read what you've got to say. Try to think up three possible titles for each of your areas of interest.

1. ....

2. ....

3. ....

Part Three – Putting It on the Net

With half the world as your market and a great title, how do you turn this into income? In Karbo's day there was no Internet and he sold by mail order. Now we can sell almost anything – on our own websites, through Amazon, eBay, Clickbank or thousands of other third-party websites. We can print our own books (one copy at a time) using print on demand sites like Café Press or Lulu. Indeed, we don't even have to print. We can sell an e-book as a pdf that is instantly created from a Word document.

Produce a short version or synopsis of your book, say just six pages, and make this available online as a pdf.

Ask your colleagues what they think. Get ideas and recommendations. Then get to work on turning this into income. Don't worry if you don't know much about websites, selling online or print on demand. If you don't have these skills, get together and work with others who do.

We will talk about working with others later, and discussing how to find people with the skills you may lack. There are many people out there who will be really keen to help you at no cost. You have the product but need the sales infrastructure; they have the sales know-how or network but no innovative products. There's an opportunity on both sides.

Books, training courses, games, information, e-books and CDs can be created from your interests. Imagine that in three years you will be famous for your knowledge. What will your product range look like, or what will your services be? In which field will you be an expert?

ANSWER

There is a big Part Four to this exercise – because from your book come speaking engagements, seminars, coaching sessions, DVDs and videos! All of these can be promoting your area of interest, expertise or experience.

Yes, your initial book can be the springboard for a range of income-generating workpieces – all in the area or topic that you enjoy and are interested in. So get moving now, if you haven't already, with looking again at Part One of this exercise: What's your passion?

GETTING TOGETHER TO CREATE WORKPIECES

Some of your workpieces may well involve forming partnerships with others. You might work with a friend on Facebook for 'Idea W', with relatives on 'Project X' and with former work colleagues on 'Initiative Y'. One activity may involve just one colleague, another several colleagues working together using online productivity tools and communicating via Skype, and a third may be three of you meeting up locally to work together.

Here are a few simple ideas to get this moving:

- Give a copy of this book to a couple of friends and then meet with them to discuss it.

- Decide to set up a new workpiece. There are no doubt lots of things you are interested in; try to find just one other person who might also be interested. Discuss your ideas. The two of you then take it forward.

- Get together (physically or online) and talk about Work It Out!. Discuss some ideas. Encourage each other and see if any potential ideas for workpieces emerge.

- Celebrate successes as workpieces are 'bolted on' for each person.

- Build your links and set common objectives.

- Create a regular routine – daily updates, weekly meetings to report on actions and success.

- Work with others to access the particular support you need, for example if one person is good with computers, or with marketing, and so on.

- Keep all workpiece options on the table for everyone, be they services, products, part-time roles, or possible businesses.

Who's on This Team?

Workpieces that involve income-generation may require help with marketing, finance advice or assistance with graphics. When the workpiece goes live you may need others to help you deliver the service, or make the products. To maximize the potential of each workpiece and get the best team on board, involve others in your plans, ask for their input and share the benefits. They will do the same for you.

Your Local Work It Out! Network

Join one or two local groups where you think you might find like-minded people. These might be the Chamber of Commerce, Golf Club, Rotary, Round Table, community group, church group, gym class, pub, book group, squash club, etc.

You could also attend classes at night school, choosing subjects such as Internet marketing, e-commerce, email marketing or self-publishing. Not only will this help you in your own efforts, but it is the ideal place to meet others who are also keen to learn about applying these techniques. This could be the start of your marketing team.

If you can't find a suitable group of local colleagues to work with, consider setting up a business group of your own. Start small, with one or two people. Tell others what you are trying to do and watch it evolve.

Remember that the aim has to be for *everyone* to be successful, so it is important to support each other, to identify possibilities and to create real workpieces for each person. Celebrate your successes, encourage each other and provide practical support.

GETTING THIS STRAIGHT: FAQS ABOUT WORK IT OUT!

Q. *Are 'workpieces' just sharing out the current jobs in a different way, ensuring everybody gets something?*

A. This is about much more than dividing up the work 'pie'. It's a fundamental shift in our thinking about work, employment and jobs. Workpieces create the opportunity to create new possibilities and explore options outside of our current job. It's about creating our own work menu. How many times have you wished that you could design your own job, work for yourself or just different people, and have greater control over your hours of work? If we are fully employed, we may have little incentive or time to do this, and of course this becomes a quality of life issue also. Those with one or two small workpieces already might easily add on a new one. They are moulding and shaping their workpieces to suit their needs, lifestyle and interests. It's a matter of empowering people to take control of their inployment, rather than holding them to ransom with the threat of being fired. We can look for workpieces in the same way as we would look for a traditional job, but also create our own workpieces with others and on our own. In this way work expands, creating wealth and wellbeing, and everyone is inployed at some level.

Q. *What about those who are unable to work?*

A. These people will no longer have the stigma of being unemployed. Everyone can make some contribution if we are creative enough and dedicated to helping them.

Q. What will job centres do?

A. They will evolve from offering full-time jobs to advising employers on new ways to define the roles they need filling, what skills are required, for how many hours and at what remuneration. They will provide help and guidance to individuals on how to link their workpieces in a practical way. Job centres will become workpiece centres. They will provide details of paid employer workpieces, voluntary workpieces and creating your own business workpieces, while drawing on and supporting local support networks.

NEED SOME GRAPHICS?

When I was writing some e-books recently I thought it would be good to have a few graphics to illustrate some of the key messages. I use the site oDesk, where you can find people all over the world who are available for assignments. The task can be worth anything from a few pounds to several hundreds. The services range from software services to help with public relations, book-keeping, legal issues, copywriting, translation, creative writing, administrative support, logo design, sales and lead generation, e-commerce, marketing, phone support and graphic design.

I listed the job 'e-book illustrations' on Monday and had 16 applications, from the US, England, China, Pakistan and India, and I offered the work to Towhid from Bangladesh on Wednesday.

This example is really important in two ways. First, you can post your requirements on these websites for free and buyers will approach you. Secondly, you can easily access the skills you need to get a workpiece moving.

CASE STUDY: KEVIN

It's All About You

I met Kevin recently, a young graphic artist who is familiar with selling services over the Internet and was using sites like oDesk, Elance, PeoplePerHour and Freelancer to try and pick up pieces of work.

He asked me how Work It Out! is different from buying and selling services in this way.

I took him back a step and asked, 'What would you really like to do?' 'I'm looking for graphic artist jobs,' he said. 'Yes' I replied, 'but if you had the choice, what sort of graphics work would you like to do?'

'I'd like to illustrate children's books,' he said

How can we make this happen? You need to find writers of children's books, send some ideas to publishers, create your website to promote your ideas, and so on.

This then becomes a workpiece: Illustrating Children's Books. It's what you want to do. You need a plan to move it forward. And you need help and support to get it to happen quickly and in the most successful way.

This is the main difference between Work It Out! and sites where you purchase or sell services. On these sites you are dependent upon someone wanting the skills (graphic work) you have and hoping that this will be close enough to your personal preferences (children's books).

DEVELOPING WORKPIECES YOU HAVE CREATED

With Work It Out! we start with our needs and work to build on them. Our efforts are concentrated on building value for ourselves rather than trawling through websites full of other people's needs.

Try and find other Work It Out! workers to provide support. You can then swap skills and time, as well as money. You can work collaboratively, helping each other to create your ideal workpieces.

Ask yourself:

- How can I build upon this?

- What could I do to make more income from this?

- Could I do this in a better or more effective way?

- If I could name three ways to make this a better workpiece, what would they be?

- What have I learned from this workpiece?

- How can my learning help others?

- If I had to sell the idea of this workpiece to others, how could I present it?

- Could I link this workpiece with something else I'm doing, or to other skills/interests I have?

- How could I link up with someone else to create something special, new, different, or more effective?

Thinking Outside the Box

It's easy to fall back into the old trap of thinking about work in terms of full-time jobs. It's easy to give up when another rejection letter arrives, or to feel trapped in a job because there is nothing better out there.

Work It Out! encourages us not to be dependent upon what happens in the old job box. Look outside the box and see what opportunities are available to create and build workpieces in the new world of work. We used to be restricted to job applications as the way to build our futures. Now we can explore a wide array of workpieces.

CRAZY LINKAGES

Map out 20 possible ideas for workpieces that are geared to moving you in the direction of where you want to be.

Don't evaluate these until you have written down all 20 ideas. Do this as quickly as you can. This exercise will develop your ability to consider your potential from a new angle, to take a fresh approach to assessing your possibilities for the future.

1. ....

2. ....

3. ....

4. ....

5. ....

6. ....

7. ....

8.

9.

10.

11.

12.

13.

14.

15.

16.

17.

18.

19.

20.

CHAPTER 5

Practical Work It Out! Skills

Here you will find out how to develop the new skills that are needed day-to-day as a Work It Out! worker. These range from developing and honing your networking skills to learning how to barter skills and resources, and summoning up the self-discipline needed to complete all your tasks. This will help you to keep driving projects forward when there is no external impetus being applied by an employer to keep you on your toes.

YOUR WORK IT OUT! TOOLKIT

What do you need in your Work It Out! toolkit?

1. An understanding of Work It Out! and the difference between looking for jobs and building workpieces.

2. A map of where you're going: What do you really want to do?

3. A view of the workpieces you'd like to build. We all start out with some workpieces, be it a job, relationships, hobbies, what have you. The task is to shape and build on this, moulding it to give you the future you want. What will you keep? What will you change and make better? Each workpiece will have an accompanying plan and, in some cases, other people who are involved in its development.

4. A team of supporters. This might be a colleague or two, friends on a social networking site, people you've found on a work site such as oDesk or Elance. It may be other Work It Out! workers. All of these can provide expertise, experience, support or

ideas to help you. As one Work It Out! worker has said, 'Why work for one person whom you may not particularly like, when you can work with ten people whom you admire and respect?'

5. A determination to get started and keep building workpieces. Self-motivation and a focus on building your future and your income are essential. You have to be determined to move each of your workpieces forward in some small way every day.

6. An acknowledgement that none of us has all the skills and experience we need, but that we can access these easily.

Work It Out! – It's Great When the Pieces Come Together

Work It Out! is about working with others so you all benefit.

Work It Out! is about workpieces coming together for added value.

Work It Out! is about others helping you to create workpieces.

Work It Out! is a solid base upon which to build your future with others.

Work It Out! – it's all about working together and helping each other

---

BARTERING METHODS AND WORK IT OUT!

Bartering is a traditional concept whereby people exchange goods and services. Indeed, before money was created, bartering was the currency of business.

A recent famous example is described in the wonderful book, *One Red Paperclip*, in which the author Kyle MacDonald charts the 14 swaps he makes as he trades up from a paper clip to a house.

Bartering is an important element of Work It Out! and can be an effective lever in accessing skills, building relationships and adding value to your workpieces.

Here are the three most common Work It Out! bartering methods:

1. **Skillswap** – for example, I might swap a driving lesson for brochure design.

2. **Timeswap** – I'll help you for three hours on X if you can help me with three hours on Y. The ratio doesn't have to be 'one for one', of course.

3. **Moneyswap** – Let's both do this at the very best Work It Out! rate we can because we are not looking to make money but to cover costs.

These three bartering methods are fully interchangeable within Work It Out!, so you can offer a service in return for time, or a great rate in return for a particular service.

Why do Work It Out! workers like bartering? Here are a few comments:

'It's just a great fun way to do business.'

'It's about relationships and helping each other to be successful rather than just money – more satisfying.'

'Bartering has helped to get any expertise when I needed [it] and didn't have the cash.'

'With bartering I've found other people in a similar position to myself [who are] trying to build a workpiece. This has given me encouragement as well as new work colleagues.'

'I feel my work is much more appreciated with bartering, than someone just paying me. It's more personal – nicer, really.'

In other words, even if you don't have much money you can still be very productive and move your workpieces forward. Just identify what skills or services you might be able to offer that could help others. And remember, helping someone else will make them keen to support you.

What help do I need with any of my workpieces?	What could I offer? – services, goods, time and great rate

A WORK IT OUT! DAILY ROUTINE

You need to have a plan for each day. Read through the following suggestions and come back to this page often as you establish your new Work It Out! daily routine.

- Move each of your workpiece ideas forward every day. Do something with each one to help create it or build it every day.

- Make your plan visible. Create an Excel spreadsheet that you update each day, stick a large piece of paper on your wall, or keep a special notebook or journal.

- Look at your plan every night and morning and ask yourself – What have I created? What new opportunity or idea have I started? Whom did I meet today to initiate something new? How did I expand or improve a workpiece that I already have?

- Be clear about your priorities for each day. Write a workpiece to-do list the evening before.

- Put a Work It Out! reminder – on your desktop, computer, the fridge door, anywhere – to remind yourself to get on with building your workpieces rather than wasting time on unproductive pottering or surfing the Net. Google has a simple little gadget that I use to help to keep me focused. It is a virtual Post-It note that sits on my screen. I use it as a reminder to get on with my workpieces, but I also find it a helpful place to jot down thoughts about particular workpieces at any time.

- Put your to-do items in order of priority and stick to it. It's too easy to spend time on your favourite tasks.

- Allocate your time effectively. Don't spend the first couple of hours answering emails from friends if this is not essential to building your workpieces.

- Be active and get things done. Work It Out! is built on small steps.

- Enjoy your success, be it creating a new workpiece, seeing a funding stream start to flow or getting income from an event you managed.

Every Hour Should Be Focused on Creating Workpieces

We can all identify with the old saying, 'Work expands to fill the time available.' How often have you worked right up to a deadline, or only finished something at the last minute? The reality is probably that you could have finished sooner. The danger is that activities imposed by others, or external events, take up most of your most precious resource: time. Spend all your time creating and building workpieces that are important to you.

So, put your workpieces first and only spend time on other activities if they are absolutely essential.

Your key task is to create potential workpieces, to get out there, physically or through the web, and meet people, to build the framework for each workpiece and to keep them all moving forward. Work It Out! really is a full-time job if you want to secure solid income quickly.

Initially you will spend all your time developing ideas and looking for opportunities, just to get your first few workpieces in place. Then as your income builds you'll spend time delivering and refining, creating better workpieces, discarding others that are no longer your priority, taking an initiative to a new level and building passive income.

SOCIAL NETWORKING

Social networking sites like Facebook and Twitter enable you to connect and communicate with people you don't know, or haven't met before, but with whom you may have something in common. Suddenly a whole world is open to us from our computer.

Work It Out! capitalizes on the major shift the Internet has wrought in the way products and services are sold. A few years ago the only way to get a sales message across was the broadcast method: adverts in magazines or at the cinema, or on billboards, television or radio. Now people are creating and selling things to each other via social networks. Each of us can sell to this marketplace. Millions of people have access to selling things to millions of people, rather than the former model where a few people – in the shape of large companies – sold things to millions of people.

One of the trailblazers of social networking, Howard Rheingold, commented recently,

You know Andy Warhol said in the future that everyone will be famous for 15 minutes, a blogger by the name of David Weinberger said 'in the future everyone will be famous for 15 people,' and I think that what we are seeing now is the technology is giving us a vast middle ground between the amateur whose parents are the only ones interested in their productions and the professional in which you have megastars.

Rheingold acknowledges

> … there is never going to be a substitute for face-to-face communication, but we have seen since the alphabet, to the telephone and now the Internet, that whenever people find a new way to communicate they will flock to it. Certainly the Internet enables you to find people that you have something in common with, that you might not have had some way of communicating with before and they might even be on the other side of the world.

From Social Networking to Self-sustainability Networking

The social networking sites Facebook, LinkedIn, Ecademy, Twitter and others are all places to find other Work It Out! workers, and create a profile showing what you can offer to others and why they should work with you, and describing what you are planning to create or build.

Social networking websites are clearly great places to link up and share ideas, while freelancing websites provide a channel to sell bits of work or pieces of our time. Both of these are important elements of Work It Out!

We now have the means to create workpieces – be it on our own or with the help and support of others. We can work, and link, and share with others to give practical as well as emotional support. We can use the power and reach of the Internet to help us to manage and achieve this. Charles Handy's concept of 'adequate money for all' can now be realized.

CASE STUDY: CHLOE

Chloe left school at 16. Although loving and supportive, her parents just weren't into education and Chloe was never pushed. She left school with a few qualifications but her real interest was in art and design. However, her grades weren't good enough to get into college.

She did a few shop jobs and came across an earlier incarnation of this book in WH Smith, where she was working at the time, when a customer asked for it.

Chloe read the book and started to think how she could get her art career moving. She approached a few charity shops and impressed them with her retail experience, enthusiasm and personality. She got a part-time job working for free which neatly fitted round her WH Smith role. Given that the charity shop was pretty quiet first thing, Chloe offered to sort out the window display. Dull and drab quickly became colourful and fun.

After a couple of months and further successes, Chloe was asked to sort out the window displays of other branches of the charity, and soon had a modest monthly contract to update all four of the windows along a similar theme. Chloe had especially wonderful displays for Easter, Christmas and Halloween.

Chloe had made an agreement that she could place a little advert on all the displays she did – 'Fabulous window displays by Chloe'. She designed a logo and produced some business cards.

On Wednesday afternoons Chloe would visit three or four small local shops and tell them about her displays, leave a business card and arrange a follow-up meeting if they were interested. Chloe quickly built up a range of monthly contracts with an optician, a cake shop and a hairdresser to do their windows.

By her eighteenth birthday Chloe had three workpieces – part-time working at WH Smith, her charity shop window displays contract, and three local shop customers. She is putting together her art portfolio and resitting her art and design exams this summer. Chloe hopes to have a new college workpiece in the autumn.

Pam's Daily Reminders

Here are the daily reminders that one successful Work It Out! worker keeps by her bed. Pam reads these every night before she goes to sleep and every morning when she wakes up, before the daily demands take over her time. Pam's view is that if she doesn't keep her plan at the forefront of her brain, other 'stuff' will take over. Now she has a rule that she doesn't spend the first hour of every day answering emails like she used to. She goes straight to her workpieces plan to see what she needs to do that day for each one.

1. My aim is to create three new workpieces by the end of March.

2. The three workpieces I will create are:
   • a web presence to sell my e-book on caring for people with Alzheimer's
   • a group of young mothers interested in getting together to look at income opportunities, and
   • a network of local shops to stock my new range of framed photos of local scenes.

3. I can access the right network of contacts and support I need to develop and build every workpiece.

4. Every day I make progress in building my workpieces.

5. I look for opportunities to help others to create and build their workpieces, and easily find others able to help me.

6. My income plan is being easily achieved through my workpieces.

You can see that some of Pam's reminders take the form of what are known as 'affirmations' – simple declarative sentences that sum up, in the present tense, our aims and ambitions. Have a think about what your personalized affirmations and reminders about your workpieces might sound like.

WORK IT OUT!: HAVE YOU GOT YOUR HEAD ROUND IT YET?

Work It Out! is a new way of thinking not just about work, but about the way that we spend our time in creating and building the workpieces that make us happy. Work It Out! puts us in control and enables us to set our own course.

The main priority, then, is to use our time effectively to create our first set of workpieces. Our focus every day will be to do something to keep each workpiece moving forward.

YOUR WORK IT OUT! JOURNAL

A Work It Out! Journal has three important elements:

1. Workpiece aims, objectives and plan

2. Record of daily outcomes

3. Income chart.

The plan for each of your workpieces needs to be updated regularly as you make progress or if unexpected things happen or you need to change your objectives for whatever reason.

So the process is:

1. Complete the first element of your journal (aims, objective and plan) for each of your workpieces.

2. Update your journal every day to monitor progress and update as necessary.

3. Update your income chart every time you earn money, secure additional revenue or win new business.

The Work It Out! Journal helps you:

- keep focused on your priorities
- record evidence that you are moving in the right direction every day
- see how far you have travelled
- prepare for being successful tomorrow.

1. WORKPIECE AIMS, OBJECTIVES AND PLAN

For each workpiece:

Aim: What are you trying to do?

Objective: How will you measure your success?

Plan: What are the key steps and timescales to achieving your objective? What resources in terms of time, money, skills, experience and so on do you need that you haven't got? How will you monitor your progress and success?

2. RECORD OF DAILY OUTCOMES

Today's activities/outcomes/follow-up for each of my workpieces

Today's date	Workpiece 1 name Notes/ Priorities for today	Workpiece 2 name Notes/ Priorities for today	Workpiece 3 name Notes/ Priorities for today	Workpiece 4 name Notes/ Priorities for today

3. INCOME CHART

Workpiece name	May				June				July			
Week	1	2	3	4	1	2	3	4	1	2	3	4
Admin role (1)				120				120				120
eBay (2)						20	30	65	124	75	45	125
Products (3)			150			150				150		
Tutoring (4)	20	20	20	40	40	40	40	40	40	60	60	60
One-off sales (5)							250					
TOTAL INCOME	**20**	**20**	**170**	**160**	**40**	**210**	**320**	**225**	**164**	**285**	**105**	**305**

Workpiece 1

I have two days' work per month which pays £60 per day. It's an administrative role for a local retailer. I am also in the process of growing this workpiece by offering my services as and when needed to other businesses. I tell them to call if and when they need me. I explain that everyone else may be looking for a job, but I am not. I am offering their business exactly what it needs.

Workpiece 2

These are my eBay sales. I list these as 10-day auctions and schedule them to finish on a Sunday evening, which is the time when most people are on the site. I usually get paid straight away into my PayPal account. I now have income every week from eBay. I find things to sell at my local market and car boot sales.

Workpiece 3

I earn £150 for every delivery of five boxes of aromatherapy candles I sell to my local shops. At present this is one sale per month, but I have the potential to expand.

Workpiece 4

This is a tutoring service I offer for £20 per session. My aim is to build up to four sessions per week.

Workpiece 5

This was a one-off sale to a local dealer of old newspapers with articles about the *Titanic* which I had collected.

CHAPTER 6

Moving Forward

Once your first workpiece is in place you need to consider what the next one will be, and to manage and develop your collection of workpieces. Some workpieces may grow, at times some will be dormant, others may be temporary, or come and go. Some workpieces will be better than others and it is valuable to assess why.

It is also important to think about branding, to give a shape, context and consistency to your workpieces.

Using income from these active workpieces, it is important to put in place 'passive' workpieces, including investments, which will generate money for a pension pot.

WHAT WILL YOUR NEXT WORKPIECE LOOK LIKE?

- What's holding you back?

- What could you add to really improve your future?

- What piece would make you happy?

Add ideas to your journal now and start tracking your progress.

WORK IT OUT! – IT'S SURPRISING HOW QUICKLY ONE WORKPIECE CAN GROW

When we start to create and build workpieces we are embarking on a process of discovery about ourselves, the new world of work and how we can build effective new relationships through the Internet. It is essential to take stock and consider where we are from time to time.

How is each workpiece doing? Do we need to change, add or get rid of anything?

There may be times when one of your workpieces will seem to take on a life of its own. The idea is working better than you could have hoped for, perhaps because of the new links you have made. When this happens, seize the opportunity to ramp up the activity and make the most of that particular workpiece. Consider how to get maximum impact. How can you create additional workpieces as a result, and use the experience to help others?

WORKPIECES ARE TEMPORARY

While it may be the case that very few people have a job for life these days, the mindset of old-style, full-time employment is something fixed and permanent.

The mindset of Work It Out! is the exact opposite. Workpieces are conceived as temporary and part of an overall mix of activities.

Workpieces are temporary for many reasons:

- Our needs change and any particular workpiece will not always be where our interests lie.

- A workpiece may not give us enough income, enjoyment or satisfaction.

- There may be other workpieces that we have created and expanded. We may still like a given workpiece, but just can't do everything and have to prioritize.

- The focus may change from income-generation to creating passive income for the future. Or we may decide to do more or less work.

- We may have discovered a new hobby or interest.

In other words, you can never think about one workpiece in isolation. Work It Out! is about the mix of workpieces and getting the right balance in terms of income, interests and enjoyment.

As you grow and circumstances change, your workpieces should also change to reflect your needs. Treat workpieces as temporary. Continually ask yourself, 'What would I really like to do?' Challenge yourself to work with new people and to create new workpieces.

WORK IT OUT! IS AN IMPERFECT PROCESS

Every idea isn't going to pan out as you might expect. Every contact isn't going to help in the way you hoped. Some ideas will flourish and grow. Others will not be worth pursuing. Some Work It Out! workers will become lifelong friends and partners, whereas others will remain contacts. Be prepared for some Work It Out! workpieces to grow easily while there are others that you just don't seem able to progress.

With the ones that do grow well, ask yourself:

• How can I leverage this success further?

• Why is it that this has worked so well?

• What lessons can I learn from what I've done?

With any that are not happening, ask yourself:

• Am I doing enough? What else could I do to get this going?

• Who could help me?

• What's the key sticking point at present? Should I restructure the idea in some way?

• Is it worth continuing with this workpiece?

Remember, all workpieces are not the same.

Typically people have one or two workpieces which provide the bulk of their income and take up the majority of their time. Then they have a few more workpieces that are important to them and enjoyable.

GENERATING PASSIVE INCOME

Passive income can be created from workpieces that continue to generate income long after you have finished the initial work.

Examples might include a property you purchased and refurbished and now let. It brings in money every month with little or no effort on your part.

Another example is where you lease a service, such as a training course that you have created, and allow others to deliver the course in their area for an annual fee.

With an eye on the future and getting older, it is important to consider how we can build some workpieces now that will create passive income streams for the future.

Here are the top 12 ways to generate passive income:

1. E-books sold automatically e.g. through Clickbank

2. License fees for using your product, method or service – e.g. your training course

3. Membership fees for joining your website, your club or your association

4. A business you created that is now effectively self-managing – e.g. you have someone who runs this business for you

5. Advertising income from your website – e.g. Google AdSense

6. Products and merchandise you created and now sell online (e.g. through Café Press)

7. Franchising your business model to others – e.g. to run in their local town

8. Automatic Internet income – e.g. through 'Site Build It!'

9. Rental income from being a landlord

10. Dividends from shares

11. Royalties from book sales or music sales or photos (e.g. online photo libraries)

12. Patent royalties from your invention, or trademark royalties from your brand.

We are used to working for an amount of time, getting paid and repeating that process. This is earned income. However, with passive income we create the asset once (e.g. e-book, property, training course, etc.) and then continue to earn money year after year from this.

You need to ensure that you are developing passive income workpieces in your collection.

CASE STUDY: JOSEPH

All Joseph ever wanted to do was to play football. He was a star at school, and as a result never concentrated much on academic work or qualifications. His ambition was to play in the Premiership but unfortunately he never quite got there and settled into a local non-league team, playing every Saturday, training on Tuesdays and Thursdays and supporting the youth team on a Sunday morning. At 28, Joseph's playing days were numbered and he was starting to worry about what he would do next.

One post-match pub conversation brought up the subject of Work It Out! and Joseph thought it might give him some ideas of what to do next. He was clear that he wanted to stay in football in some way if he could. Joseph approached his own club and asked if they would sponsor him to do his UEFA coaching licence, as this was an obvious route into football training, or even management. Joseph paid his own fees out of his weekly appearance money and worked for the club for free on a Local Authority scheme for youngsters during the summer months.

It was during these months that Joseph built up some good links with grateful parents, one of whom worked for the local newspaper. He asked if Joseph would be interested in writing a short review of the under-14 league games every week. He hadn't done anything like this before, but the sports editor was glad to have original reporting and was happy to re-work Joseph's initial pieces. He told the game from a footballer's perspective and 'Joseph's Corner' became a regular feature on page 31. He reckons that Sky Sports is just around the corner!

Joseph's workpieces now include working for his UEFA 'A' and 'B' badges, his weekly sports reporting and his summer work with the Local Authority, which has now expanded into school initiatives during term time. What's more, he's just been asked to become Assistant Manager of the under-18s club team.

YOU ARE YOUR BRAND(S)

Every person can develop a brand to give shape, context and substance to what they offer.

'Sparkling Windows' is much more appealing than 'John Smith window cleaner'. A 'window' logo could be added. A silver and blue colour scheme would help to imprint the brand in people's minds.

The other key point about your brands – yes, you can have more than one! – is that these are entities that can be developed and perhaps, eventually, sold.

Make sure you have a good dot.com name for each brand, so that each element can build its own online presence. The web immediately gives international exposure to workpieces we wish to promote, and there are plenty of free and low-cost services for developing websites.

Workpieces can also be promoted through contacts on Facebook, LinkedIn, Ecademy, Twitter and so on.

Be clear about how you want people to react to your website. Think about the following points:

- Do you want people to sign up for your special e-book?

- Do you want them to purchase your new product or service?

- Do you want them to become a member?

- Do you want them to help you with ideas, skills, time or resources?

Six Ways to Build Your Brands Quickly

1. Build a web presence: Just type 'free website' into Google and have fun trying out one or two website-building options. If you can use the Internet, you can easily build a good-looking website.

2. Go niche – be specific about exactly what your site is about and what you want it to achieve.

3. Get a good dot.com. Most of the obvious dot. com names are gone but here are two ways to find your ideal name: a) Put two or three words together that summarize what your site is about (comparethemarket or lastminute are famous examples of this); b) Create a new 'made up' word along the lines of eBay or Expedia. Make it easy to remember and you're halfway there!

4. Choose a colour scheme.

5. Design a logo.

6. Update your content every day, and communicate regularly with your subscribers or email contacts.

WHAT'S YOUR NEXT BRIGHT IDEA?

Take a fresh look at each of your workpieces and ask yourself

- What could I do to really get this moving forward?

- What would others do in my place?

- What would I suggest to someone else who asked me for advice in making this better?

Try and write down a range of ideas to boost the development of each of your workpieces, then choose the one you think is the best.

CHAPTER 7

The Work It Out! Extended Family

Losing a job may also mean an instant end to the camaraderie and social connections of the workplace, but Work It Out! provides the framework to build a circle of contacts and like-minded people. Even when sitting in front of your computer at home, trying to create and progress workpieces, you are not alone. This chapter shows you how to draw on the skills of others, how to help them in return and how to build teams to deliver particular workpieces. It ends with a checklist that will help ensure that your communications network is robust.

FRIENDSHIP AND COMPANIONSHIP

One of the most difficult consequences of unemployment is losing the day-to-day chat and friendships that existed at work.

Work It Out! puts this back – and more. It recognizes that new teams, networks and partners have to be available immediately.

The typical entrepreneurs may be used to working on their own, but they do create their own support network over time. Even so, entrepreneurship can be primarily quite a lonely business. With inployment, however, 'co-workers' are key. They provide the mutually reinforcing encouragement and daily reminders of priorities that are so essential.

- What input or support do you need for each of your workpieces?

- Who can help you and how will you find them?

- Whom can you support?

Remember:

- **Work It Out! workers are flexible and adaptable. They look at the bigger picture of relationship-building and opportunity-creation – rather than just their own short-term gain.**

- **Work It Out! is a lifelong process. Every contact and conversation is an investment in your future. You might only work with someone once, or on many workpieces together. You will often become friends in the proper sense of the word.**

- **Work It Out! is all about working together and helping each other.**

YOU ARE NOT ALONE

Job-search or business start-up can often be solitary – each of us trying as best we can to make that next move happen.

Work It Out! however, is rooted in a vast web of mutually supportive interactions and activities rather than a solitary path. This fabric of social interaction is important because:

- It provides additional resources and expertise to help each of us create ideas and develop workpieces.

- It provides a positive critique for each of us of what could work, how to make an idea better, or what is likely to take a lot of time for little return.

- It provides encouragement, friendship and support.

- It provides a regular focus for getting things done and meeting deadlines. For example, if you know that you are going online with two colleagues to discuss Project X on Friday, then you should be keen to have your tasks completed. If you know that someone is waiting on your input, then you're far more likely to get it done.

- It provides a platform for problem-solving. If you are stuck or need advice or support, then the Work It Out! network can offer this.

OUR BIG EXTENDED FAMILY

Many networks on the web are established as online communities where people can meet each other, interact and build links. Work It Out! however, is more like an extended family than an online community.

Work It Out! is dealing with serious and important situations – the quality of people's lives can be dependent upon their ability to make ends meet and create a solid future for themselves and their families. This doesn't mean it isn't fun and exciting – it has to be. But underpinning our efforts has to be a level of commitment more akin to that in a family set-up than a general community.

Work It Out! rests on a set of values that are integral to the process. We make things happen and get things done, with and through others. Our success is due in some part to working with others and the support, guidance and advice they provide. Business and income-generation do not exist in a vacuum. Good business ideas are rooted in reality and sit comfortably in our own real-life situations.

CASE STUDY: BOB

Bob is 42 years old and an only child. His father died when he was 20. Recently his mother has been diagnosed with multiple sclerosis and now requires round-the-clock support. Up to this point, Bob had a successful career as an accountant with a supermarket chain, but he decided that there was no alternative but to resign from his full-time work and become his mother's full-time carer.

The various allowances Bob received as a carer were only just sufficient to keep himself and his mother in food and accommodation. Over time, Bob also missed the day-to-day camaraderie of his work colleagues and felt isolated at home. The only time he met people was when he went shopping.

One day when Bob was out, he met one of his ex-colleagues who asked how he was getting on. Bob's friend recommended that he check out Work It Out! on the Internet as he thought it might provide some options, possibly including doing part-time work from home.

Bob realized that with his finance experience and skills plus some additional support, he could, amongst other things, provide a personal tax-consulting service from home.

Bob approached his old company, which was happy for him to offer his services to employees. They also asked if he would fill in and provide some part-time accounting support for holiday cover, maternity leave and other absences, delivered from home on an as-needed basis. Within three weeks Bob had a new tax business, an ad-hoc finance support role and regular contact with his ex-colleagues. His mother was still the priority, but now he had some other things to do as well, and that seemed to help them both.

FAMILY RULES OK

Here are a few guidelines to help when you're working with other Work It Out! workers:

1. When starting to develop ideas and opportunities together, be clear about the arrangement – define the exchange, timescales and what you all hope/ expect to get out of it.

2. Don't waste other people's time.

3. Always answer an email from a fellow Work It Out! worker. Your words of support or encouragement might just be the spark someone needs. If you are unable to help then explain why and maybe suggest other ideas.

4. Likewise, don't send unnecessary emails (spam).

5. Be happy to ask for help and be equally happy to be asked.

6. Give positive feedback on those that help you. Tell your other colleagues how a piece of advice or assistance made something happen.

WHO CAN YOU HELP TODAY?

Work It Out! workers don't wait to be asked, they look for ways to help others create, manage or build their workpieces. Often this can be a question of simply asking how things are, or sharing advice and information about a new website maybe. Such kindnesses lead to collaboration, and to new business. A network of strong, supportive colleagues is created, new relationships and friendships are formed and income flows.

For this reason it's OK for Work It Out! workers to ask for help and advice. In fact, it's an essential part of the relationship-building process.

So, connect and create workpieces with others.

• Who is going to work with you on your latest workpiece?

• How will you link up with them?

• Who is going to do which elements?

A QUICK WORK IT OUT! COMMUNICATION AUDIT

Email

- How many of the emails that you sent out today were about moving your workpieces forward?

- How many of the emails you received today helped you to move your workpieces forward?

Text

- How many of the texts that you sent today were about moving your workpieces forward?

- How many of the texts you received today helped you to move your workpieces forward?

Social Networking

- How many of the last postings you sent/ received on your favourite social networking site were about moving your workpieces forward?

Work It Out! Communication Score Card

	Sent for work-pieces	Sent for other	% Work It Out!	Received for work-pieces	Received for other	% Work It Out!
Emails						
Texts						
Social networking						
Total						

Complete this audit once a day to help keep your communication focused. There is so much competition for our time, and so many demands on our attention, that this is a good way of keeping track and ensuring workpieces are moving forward.

CHAPTER 8

Work It Out! for All Ages

If full-time employment is a thing of the past, the education and training of young people needs to reflect this. This chapter considers the changes that are needed in schools to prepare our children for the new world of work, and considers new model apprenticeships for Work It Out! workers.

MANY PATHS AND MANY OPPORTUNITIES

Learning is a lifelong process. New technology and advances in science, health and environmental issues spur our interest and challenge us to find out more. Wherever our interests and concerns are, they should and can be the inspiration for learning and may also, in some small way, contribute to the learning of those around us.

Within Work It Out! none of us follows one career path any more. We can try out other roles and have two or three workpieces on the go at the same time. It is possible to merge informal learning seamlessly into our daily routine. In this way we don't get stuck in a rut or waste time in a job we've grown tired of. If it's not right, or doesn't suit us, we change it or create anew.

In general we are living longer and healthier lives and staying active longer. It may be an off-putting thing to say, but the Work It Out! Way of life continues right up until we die. We will always be involved in some activities, have areas of interest and have something that we enjoy. Work may be about money for many people, but Work It Out! is about all of life's activities.

The traditional career model was linear. We trod a recognized path from school, to training, to job, to retirement:

School→training/college→job→unemployed→job→retirement

The Work It Out! model goes more like this:

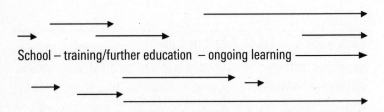

School – training/further education – ongoing learning

Work It Out! activities start at school. This is where we learn it is the norm to do more than one thing with our lives. We can be in different roles at different times. We can add to and change what we are.

We can also learn at school that we are in charge of this process. From the age of six or seven we can begin to create ideas and develop projects, be it fundraising for the school or for local charities, helping to run the school shop, organizing parents' events or setting up mini-businesses making and selling arts and crafts at the school bazaar or sports day. Each of these activities offers the opportunity to learn essential project-management skills which will last our whole lives.

These kinds of interests also equip us to work effectively in teams and understand the different roles and skills that are involved – be they creative, practical, about time-keeping or about being organized. We learn to work with others, listen to their ideas, deal with disputes, present our ideas and make something happen. These are the core building blocks of the personal effectiveness and interpersonal skills that are so essential to Work It Out!

LESSONS – OLD AND NEW

Old Lesson

Don't chop and change jobs – you won't be seen as reliable.

New Lesson

Do change and adapt – you'll be flexible and successful.

Old Lesson

Get good qualifications and you will get a good job.

New Lesson

Learn about Work It Out! and start creating some workpieces now.

CREATING WORKPIECES AT SCHOOL

Schools already provide many of the ingredients for learning the essential skills for the new world of work. The network of fellow students is already there. The IT infrastructure is available. The skills and personal support of teachers can facilitate this process. Children can learn from a whole variety of activities, including voluntary work, small business projects, Fairtrade events, school plays, overseas trips and so on.

While many schools are doing much of this, there is a difference in emphasis once these activities are seen in the context of Work It Out! The real benefit comes when they are viewed in terms of their relationship to the new world of work, and when children appreciate that skills they are developing in an activity are important in their future inployment lives.

WORK IT OUT! – IT'S CHILD'S PLAY

Children are natural Work It Out! workers. They move effortlessly between activities and will devote huge amounts of time to an activity that they are enjoying, be it playing house, looking after a new pet, watching a TV programme or playing football or a computer game. Have you noticed how happy and excited they can become over the simplest activity or event? It is important to cherish and encourage this interest and, as adults, to learn from it.

WHAT'S HAPPENING WITH TEACHING?

In the context of Work It Out!, homework is not just more of what has taken place in class, but tries to encourage the practical application of new information or skills – through projects, teamwork and joint assignments.

Homework or 'projectwork' should be pupil-led – not teacher-directed. The responsibility shifts to the pupils to work together to produce results. This encourages the development of goal-setting, planning, relationship- and team-building skills.

Teachers are the key to making inployment training effective. They will themselves need training and support on the methodology as it applies to young people and their development needs. It may also be necessary to update their technical skills, facilitation skills, and project-management and marketing skills.

Teachers don't have to wait, though; they can start to develop Work It Out! with their students right now by introducing the idea of creating and building workpieces and encouraging the development of project-management skills.

THE SCHOOL ASSETS

In the new world of work, schools need to rethink the policy of closing at 3:30 p.m. and being closed all weekend. There is little point having valuable resources lying unused at the very time when pupils could benefit from them to help develop their workpieces.

In all of this there is a need to rethink the links between school, work and personal success. New approaches, different staffing and resourcing models and a different mode of thinking will characterize those schools that are best equipped to meet the needs of pupils as they are shaped for the new world of work.

The link between parents and teachers can be more effective in promoting a child's strengths and interests through the development of workpieces, in particular if these fall outside the traditional curriculum subjects (like song-writing or writing and producing e-books, film-making or photography, growing vegetables, etc.).

Outside formal teaching hours, school can provide a safe environment in which to learn project-management, team-working, production and marketing skills. Imagine groups of children and young people having fun developing their workpieces, and seeing and learning from what others are doing. In this scenario Work It Out! becomes a key component of learning – thereby making the transition to the new world of work seamless. Young people will already have created workpieces that generate income and give enjoyment.

In the formal classroom setting, this can be supported not just by teachers but also older pupils. This in turn will enhance the older students' personal development through having responsibility for mentoring or coaching younger groups. Older pupils also learn to work with teachers in a more mature way than the traditional teacher-pupil relationship – thereby developing their research and problem-solving skills and engendering a 'making-it-happen' mentality.

WORK IT OUT! SKILLS – LEARNING AND DOING

The current education systems tend to be polarized between academic achievement and vocational training. Those with the aptitude for exams do fact-based learning, the rest are taught vocational skills. Despite attempts to acknowledge this distinction and turn it to advantage, there remains a divide between academic and vocational, and between school and the world of work. While clever children get work placements with professional firms, those in the lower sets are likely to be stacking supermarket shelves.

Work It Out! recognizes that we all need a mix of learning and doing to be successful. We have to be able both to think through how to take on and execute a project, and then get out there and make it happen. Thinking and doing are complementary and essential elements.

Whatever our individual intellectual:practical bias may be, Work It Out! recognizes the need to source more information than we currently possess, and access skills we do not already have. The three Cs – communication skills, a confident approach and clarity of purpose – are the new mantra of teaching. Clarity of purpose comes from knowing our objectives. A confident approach comes from an understanding of the Work It Out! ethos. Communication skills are developed in creating and building new workpieces.

Key Points

- Homework should evolve to 'project work' and onto Work It Out!

- There should be a Work It Out! 'lesson' incorporated into the curriculum, or time every day to create and build workpieces. This can be during or after the traditional school day.

- There should be recognition and celebration of Work It Out! success, creativity and achievements, as in the case of new products, voluntary work, recycling initiatives, healthy eating initiatives, information for school websites, contributions to local papers, etc.

- There is a need to rethink how best to support teachers in all of this. Perhaps there is a role for retired businesspeople who can act as facilitators? Perhaps parents should be encouraged to share their skills, experience and interests on a more structured basis, working with small groups?

This is not about an overnight revolution. It is about gently building awareness within each school about the new world of work, and allowing teachers to explore the opportunities to enhance our children's education and future.

FURTHER EDUCATION AND WORK IT OUT!

There may be opportunities for employers in both the private and public sectors to join forces with Further and Higher Education providers in new and creative ways through Work It Out!, resulting in a more integrated approach to linking education and work.

At the present time, third-level education, the workplace and students all largely inhabit their own separate worlds. There would be benefits if workpieces could be applied to provide students with greater practical experience, to enable employers to focus students on real-world scenarios, and for universities and colleges to develop a more holistic approach to learning.

If students are expected to build some workpieces relating to their specialisms, then:

1. The transition to the real world could already be established *before* graduation.

2. Employers would have a pool of potential skills and future employees.

3. Colleges and universities could link academic work, research and workpieces.

4. Students would have the opportunity to learn from the case-study experiences of their peers.

Workpieces could, of course, go well beyond the traditional work experience model, by including specific project work, tackling current challenges and exploring options for product or service development. Students could be enabled to make a real contribution through the support of employers, peers and teachers.

Given that students and college or university staff will be contributing to the future of the labour market, it seems appropriate that employers should make some payment, to be split between the college and students perhaps. Employers may baulk at this, but the fact is that student workpieces will be of value.

Workpieces could also form part of academic assessment, providing clear evidence of how well a student can apply his or her knowledge in the workplace. Unlike most traditional projects, workpieces can provide the opportunity to make assessments of a student's organizational abilities, academic progress and personal development.

As an example, a local small business could engage students to support its market research, product development or online presence, all activities for which there is likely to be little time in-house. Similarly, students could be encouraged to promote community wellbeing, providing exercise and healthy eating plans for schools or researching the delivery of services for the elderly in their homes.

If every organization had the opportunity to identify the skills it needed and suggest student workpieces for acquiring these skills, students could acquire a wealth of experience in the real world of work.

CASE STUDY: SHIRLEY

Shirley is 33 years old and has built a successful career as a web designer with a major web design company. Since she turned 30, however, she has become increasingly unhappy and unfulfilled at work. She continues to complete all her projects on time and has received very positive reviews of her work, but it's not what she really wants to do.

Shirley found Work It Out! through Facebook and quickly realized its value. Here was a business network that would enable her to analyse her skills, competencies and abilities, helping her to identify a new path that would allow her to earn sufficient income while doing work in which she is really interested.

After investigating Work It Out! in more detail, Shirley realized what she really wanted to do was to create and launch her own hair-piece and wig business for people who lose their hair as a consequence of radiotherapy treatment for cancer. Shirley remembered how her own mother had suffered years before, and how it had left a deep impression on her.

Shirley began to identify some contacts, including people who provide similar services in other parts of the world, though her networking links. She carried out research with friends, a local cancer unit, local suppliers and patients. It was challenging and exhausting in every way, but one of the most satisfying things that Shirley had undertaken for a long time.

Her web experience was at the fore when she subsequently launched an online haircare service for cancer patients worldwide. Her free e-book, packed with advice and case studies, had over 3,000 downloads in the first six months. The business is flying, but the thing that really matters to Shirley is the feedback from patients, who report they now have the confidence to go out again.

Shirley now has three workpieces: web design work, which she does on a freelance basis for a few clients, an online haircare business and, much to her surprise, she is an author. Her e-book was published in paperback recently.

WORK IT OUT! APPRENTICE – YOU'RE HIRED

The idea of working with others in a mutually supportive relationship in order to become successful is not new. The concept of one or more experienced people spending years mentoring, training and advising others while working and earning is at the heart of the traditional apprenticeship system. Close relationships were developed between craftsman and apprentice – often lasting a lifetime.

The apprenticeship is one of the few remaining links to the pre-Industrial Revolution era of the artisan. It was based on the commitment by an apprentice for a minimum time period, depending on the trade or profession, of perhaps five to seven years (though modern apprenticeships are shorter, at three years). This allowed apprentices to develop, learn and practise under the guidance, direction and supervision of qualified craftspeople. Typically, apprentices would receive no, or very low pay.

Acceptance into the guild or profession on completion of an apprenticeship was dependent not only on demonstration of the required proficiency, but also integrity and commitment to the ongoing development of skills and competencies, and the promotion of the standards of the guild or profession.

In Ireland, for example, the crafts were held in very high esteem. In particular, the craft of the mason is preserved and immortalized in Irish mythology in the person of the *Gobán Saor*, a master builder who went about the country building *Dúns* (forts) and fortresses for the *Ríthe* (kings) and *Árd Ríthe* (high kings). The *Gobán* was not only a master craftsman, but also something of a *Seannachaí* (storyteller) and philosopher. He is credited with the origin of the proverb *Giorraíonn beirt bóthar* or 'Two shorten the road.'

The story goes that one day as the *Gobán* and his son set off on a long journey he turned to his son and asked him to shorten the road. The puzzled son responded that neither he nor anybody else could make the road shorter than it was. *Gobán* told him if he didn't shorten the road they were going back home. Which they duly did. The following morning they set off again and the same thing happened. That evening the exasperated son sought advice from his mother. The following morning when they set off yet again, *Gobán* asked his son to shorten the road. This time, the son replied, 'Once upon a time ...' And they continued on their journey.

The traditional apprenticeship system is now evolving within Work It Out!. The process is not as formal, nor are there indentures that require people to tie themselves to a single master. Now those wanting to learn new skills can find more than one person to guide them, and can access their skills and experience via the Internet.

CHAPTER 9

Work It Out! and HR

It's important to think of Work It Out! as relevant to more than just the unemployed. It is also critical to the way in which companies are run and organized, and how they access skills and resources. Over the past 15 years many companies have come to appreciate the flexibility that outsourcing can provide, and now many are looking to establish this flexibility in-house as well. It becomes a significant new duty for Human Resources teams to reflect this in the way people are managed. The move to Work It Out! provides trades unions with the opportunity to take the initiative and support members and recruits who are performing workpieces for more than one employer.

WORK IT OUT! IS THE NEW WORKPLACE

Instead of going to a factory or office and spending all of our working time there, we can now use the Work It Out! approach as the basis for setting priorities, creating income opportunities and managing our activities.

This doesn't mean being online all the time or running loads of businesses. It means linking up with others, sharing ideas and getting input, and building workpieces. This is very different from the workplace of the past, where we were told where to go and what to do. The organizational structure is now based around us. We are in charge of our activities and income and, with the help of others, we can create the structure to support this.

Every time you sit down at your computer it should be with the intention of building your workpieces. Whom do I need to chase up? What's the next step with this? How can I find someone to help with that?

Your computer is effectively your workplace. Before we may have gone to the factory or the office to work. Now technology allows us to take our workplace with us. But, as at the office and factory, our aim is to produce and to earn.

WORKPIECES ARE THE NEW HR SPECIALISM

Like the legislation around health and safety, employment or equality before it, Work It Out! and workpieces are emerging as the next specialism and innovation in Human Resource Management.

And HR Management is exactly what we are talking about: how we can best manage our human resources, not from the traditional perspective of fixed full-time employees, but from the vantage point of the potential benefits of flexible workpieces created to suit the individual and the employer.

The old employer–employee relationship has already become blurred around the edges as more and more work is undertaken through part-time roles, temping, ad-hoc assignments, home-based activities, outsourcing, online work, freelancing, project work and so on. Up to now these have not been labelled as such, but they are all examples of workpieces.

The old single employment contract is no longer appropriate. Now we work under informal mutual responsibility agreements. The priority is to get a piece of work completed, whether it be in two hours, tomorrow or over the next two years, at the right cost, to the correct standard and in the best way.

Employers and HR specialists are increasingly defining work in terms of tasks to be done. Whereas work was traditionally allocated on a full-time basis, a task (aka workpiece) may for example be 60 hours over six weeks. Pay could then be based on outcomes and/ or time spent.

This immediately raises two questions:

1. Can employers continue to afford the cost and inflexibility of all work being packaged into full-time roles?

2. Could public services improve their efficiency and effectiveness if they adopted some aspects of Work It Out! in their procurement procedures?

Workpiece development is likely to become a central and integral part of the functions of HR. The ability to analyse an organization's work requirements already exists in the shape of delivery targets. It is no longer appropriate to respond to these by creating full-time jobs. There is a whole array of different relationships – defined by outputs, rewards, recognition and roles – available through effective workpiece design.

As individual Work It Out! workers, we will all become workpiece designers, learning to drill down to the key skills and experience needed to deliver a particular product or service. As managers and employees, we will learn how to design workpieces that get the work done effectively and at the lowest cost.

This mode of working is more inclusive, giving organizations the ability to design workpieces that meet the employment needs of everyone, from young people, to home workers and people with disabilities.

Beyond the design of individual workpieces, it will be necessary to manage the interaction between and across workpieces, building a shared pool of knowledge out of each individual's workpiece experience.

Using networking and collaboration tools it will be possible to respond to the organizational needs and environment in a more dynamic and effective way. It will no longer be a case of the need for additional work being identified, followed by the laborious writing of job specifications and descriptions, organizing press advertising, waiting for responses, application sifting, interviewing and waiting for the applicant's availability, which can take anything from 4 to 12 weeks, or longer. Those days are gone. Through an array of websites like oDesk, Elance and PeoplePerHour it is possible to find suitably qualified and experienced workers within a couple of hours, to do a specific piece of work.

It is possible to identify the work needed, design the workpieces, put these on the Internet, receive applications online, even interview online, for example, using Skype or a webcam, in a matter of days, not months. Remember, workpieces can be shaped in line with the skills and competencies available. We don't have to trade off candidate A with candidate B, or settle for someone who offers only 90 per cent of the qualifications needed. In the old days, Candidate A may have had good qualifications but limited relevant experience, while Candidate B may have had really good experience but no formal qualifications. An employer would have had to choose between these candidates, trading experience for qualifications or vice versa. With Work It Out! we can have the best of both candidates by creating workpieces to suit each person. The employer gets maximum experience and the best qualifications, and both candidates get a great new workpiece.

HR departments need to be conversant with the tools that are available for configuring and analysing data in line with an organization's needs – for example, cost savings, absenteeism, failure to meet standards, new product development. They should evaluate the effectiveness of different workpiece structures and formats for their organization in terms of productivity gains, added value and impact on the bottom line. HR departments are well placed to be the engine for driving this new layer of organizational learning across functions, departments, locations and services/products.

In the traditional environment, HR is situated in a quiet suburban administrative cul-de-sac. It is just about to be relocated to the city centre. Whereas HR may have been a passive support function, it is now set to become a central value-adder. The opportunities of Work It Out! and the availability of individuals to take on myriad workpieces – combined with Internet technology and data management – provides a whole new context for the traditional HR role in promoting organizational effectiveness, adding value and creating work opportunities.

THE OPPORTUNITY FOR TRADE UNIONS

Trade unions are clearly at the forefront of this changing world of work, finding a wider potential membership base and developing a new range of support services for members.

The key priority will no longer be about protecting individual rights with one employer, but supporting individuals across a number of employers and in a range of different work-based situations.

Unions that are able to see beyond the traditional full-time employer–employee model will recognize that there is the potential to leverage their members' expertise and effectiveness across the whole population, rather than just a segment, through Work It Out! Here are a few questions to consider:

- How can the collective strength of the Trade Union movement support and assist people in the new world of work?

- How can the expertise of individual unions engage a wider audience and help to create additional perspectives and opportunities for workpiece development (say, for example, in engineering)?

- How can unions offer expertise and add value for Work It Out! workers
  - individually across different workpieces?
  - in ad-hoc and temporary arrangements with employers?
  - in helping to support the development of effective new working relationships?

REDUNDANCY, RESTRUCTURING, RETIREMENT AND REORGANIZATION

One of the most difficult situations for any employee who has been in the same organization for many years is when he or she has to stop working. With redundancy or retirement, the working environment can instantly disappear. Friends and colleagues are no longer there; the routine and support structure that come with being employed are gone. And the prospect is that all of this comes with little or no money, and an uncertain future.

It would be better if the relationships built up over years with colleagues within an organization could be transformed, rather than just ended abruptly. Employers considering making people redundant, looking at restructuring, planning for early retirements or looking at reorganizing the business have an opportunity to provide a Work It Out! platform for employees who may be affected.

Some organizations have already set up an internal Work It Out! process, allowing employees to learn about the new world of work and create workpieces over a six-month period. The aim is that by the end of six months each person will be capable of becoming sustainable, with a range of workpieces in place.

The key to reducing the trauma of losing a job is to begin the process early, so that in effect one's current job becomes the first workpiece. As this winds down, new workpieces start to be added and relationships with colleagues are transformed rather than broken off.

ALTERNATIVES TO REDUNDANCY

Alternatives to Redundancy (ATR) schemes have become increasingly popular during the current financial crisis, as employers have sought ways to reduce costs while maintaining the work force.

ATR schemes may encompass different things, such as extended holidays/unpaid leave, temporary lay-offs, reduced hours, salary/wage cuts or working without pay for a month. These are examples of how employers are trying to restructure traditional jobs to make them more responsive to the business and the economy. But while ATR schemes on their own may be just delaying the inevitable redundancy situation, an ATR scheme based on Work It Out! can be the launch-pad for a new career. Drawing on resources in the workplace, and on each other, employees can use their unpaid leave to create new workpieces together.

WORKPIECES FOR THE OVER-50S

Many people at 50 or approaching 60 or 65 are not in a position, either mentally or materially, to stop working even though they may want to ease off a bit or perhaps do different things. We will have different workpieces as our circumstances change, and these may include a personal project, travel, spending time with grandchildren, a few hours' consultancy, voluntary work, writing, and so on. Indeed, over the next 10 to 20 years, greater life expectancy and the demographic shift that will come as the baby boomers reach retirement age will put an incredible strain on the pensions system and Government resources.

One reality of the new world of work is that retirement is no longer a realistic concept. The idea that we drop everything when we get to 65 seems a bit silly these days. And the hope that we will get enough money from the state and private pensions to do all we want, pay medical bills, travel, help our families and so on, is increasingly unrealistic.

Being over 60 is just another phase of our lives, in which we should be able to set our own priorities and have the income we need. Creating our own income sources for retirement well before we get to 60 or 65 is therefore a priority.

Financial security in old age used to involve saving for a pension, but as recent experience shows, we can no longer trust banks, Government or financial institutions to look after our money and guarantee returns. As we get older our work will reflect a different set of skills, encompassing how and where to invest, how to manage income from investments and create passive income-generation. These are workpieces that should be put in place now, not just as we approach retirement age. And they are workpieces that we need to direct and control.

However, it remains the case that everyone will not be in a position to put such retirement workpieces in place, and the Government will have to create a new infrastructure to replace the increasingly outdated retirement and pensions model. Simply extending the retirement age and making us all work longer will not suffice.

In inployment, with the support of others and different workpieces, you can create a mixture of income streams. You can then ease off as you get older, choosing your workpieces to match your energy levels.

Certainly, the old model of having a job one day and then no job when you turn 65 is crumbling. People are keen to keep busy and active after retiring. They want to use their skills, make a contribution, give something back or carry on earning. Many enjoy the social aspect of working, the thought of a new challenge or the opportunity to earn some extra cash.

Workpieces provide the ideal framework for those approaching retirement. A gradual retirement period, over say two years, provides us with an opportunity to adjust to having extra time and to create and build other workpieces.

CASE STUDY: JOHN

John is 63 years old and soon to retire from his job as an insurance assessor for a major insurance company. He has been looking forward to this as an opportunity to use his pension to do voluntary work in Africa. This has been on his mind ever since he completed a sponsored climb of Mount Kilimanjaro in 2004 when he visited some of the orphanages that were to benefit from his fundraising. The experience inspired him to resolve that when it was financially possible, he would return as a volunteer and give something back.

John was made redundant in the recession in the 1980s, and since then has been on a defined contribution scheme with his present employer. Unfortunately, the current recession has resulted in the pension fund being reduced by almost 50 per cent. Even combined with the State pension, this is not enough to retire on. It certainly would not allow him to do the volunteering work.

While John was trying to work out how to achieve his retirement plan, he came across Work It Out! He liked the idea of a web-based network enabling people to support each other in developing sustainable income streams through workpieces. What made John sit up and take notice, however, was that one of the workpieces used in an online example was of doing voluntary work relating to projects in Africa. John quickly resolved to identify workpieces that would give him the income he needed to fund voluntary work and at the same time make good the shortfall in his pension.

John soon saw an opportunity for his first workpiece. Not far from where he lived, every Sunday from 6 a.m. there was a huge car boot sale which attracted people from across the region. He checked out eBay to see what type of products sold well, and for what prices, and started visiting the car boot sale to find things he felt he could sell for a good profit. He devoted Sunday afternoons to cleaning, photographing and posting the items he had purchased. Very quickly, this business started delivering a good income stream, and meanwhile he still had his full-time job.

In the process of selling on eBay, John became a specialist on pub memorabilia. Old bottles, labels and signs were just a few of the items he sold. Buyers were keen to get more items, and he built up a good network of customers. John then asked his Work It Out! contacts for ideas on how he could source more products and started to develop some ideas with the help of Andy in Scotland, who knew about merchandising. Together they created their own product range of postcards, mugs and t-shirts for their new eBay shop.

By the time of John's retirement the pub memorabilia business had grown significantly and Andy was running this full time. The additional income, coupled with the flexibility of time, enabled John to achieve his dream and spend four months a year doing volunteer work in southern Ethiopia in conjunction with a local organization.

John and Andy have now expanded the product range to include calendars, old style prints and stationery, and John has his retirement workpieces in place: his pension, his memorabilia business and his charity work.

WORK IT OUT! IS ESSENTIAL FOR THOSE IN FULL-TIME EMPLOYMENT

Work It Out! is important for everyone, not just those out of work or facing retirement. But for those in work who want to build up workpieces, the challenge is finding time to do so. Here are some suggestions for those in full-time employment on how to get started:

- Train yourself in Work It Out!

- Think about your current role, your future plans and what else you really want to do.

- Begin to focus your free time on beginning to create other workpieces.

- Look at how your organization can change the way it buys services and goods to assist those looking to add a workpiece.

BECOME A WORKPIECE DEVELOPMENT SPECIALIST

Maybe you have found a workpiece that's of little interest to you but may suit someone else, or have created a workpiece that could be replicated in other areas, and would like to find others to help you with doing this.

Work It Out! provides everyone with the opportunity to identify workpieces, whether for themselves or others. The critical requirement for doing so is to shift the old mindset and keep your mind open to the possibility of new workpieces.

CHAPTER 10

An End to Unemployment

The Government is running to catch up. We are still in a full-time jobs culture and Government policies are out of kilter. Rather than job creation focusing solely on funding initiatives by companies, it should support individuals in learning the skills of Work It Out! and helping them to become self-reliant.

WORK IT OUT! AND UNEMPLOYMENT

As so often happens when there is a large-scale change in society, the Government is running to catch up and make an adequate response. Full-time employment in the traditional sense, with all the trimmings of pensions and so on, may be on the way out. But we are still living in the full-time jobs culture. As a result the Government is still basing policies for the unemployed on the idea of full-time employment, rather than moving forward on the basis of Work It Out! and individual potential.

This requires a radically different approach and a comprehensive shift in thinking, policy and programmes for the jobless. Governments should now be considering how best to support individuals to 'skill-up' for Work It Out!

CHANGE YOUR ROLE FROM EMPLOYEE TO WORK IT OUT! WORKER

During the last recession, when I set up my first training business, I knew I had to focus on where the opportunities were. At the time the Government was determined to reduce unemployment figures by sending people on training schemes, and thus getting them off the unemployment register.

Many unemployment training providers were offering schemes based around environmental/conservation projects, such as cleaning up wasteland, with some job-search training in the local community centre. We took the view that unemployed people needed the best support available to get back to work. Rather than schemes that would fill their time and maybe have some positive effects in terms of the local environment, we focused on the outcome, which was to help people to get qualifications and find jobs. We provided the best trainers and professional resources and settings. And we judged our success, not in terms of how many courses we ran or how many people we processed through them (and therefore what our company turnover was), but on success for those we were working with. The expectation of individuals who came on our courses was not that they were there to fill in time, but that they were there to work hard. In return we did all we could to help them to be successful.

When the business was sold some years later it was delivering 4,000 accredited qualifications every year and getting 5,000 people into full-time employment (as it was in those days) through a national network of 10 training centres. All this was possible simply by changing the roles and expectations placed on an unemployed person. We provided a structure and support, but they made the opportunity work for themselves.

Similarly, Work It Out! involves changing roles. Dealing with unemployment or redundancy should not be a solitary task, but a team effort. Anyone in this position should not be left sitting at home feeling despondent and wondering what to do. Rather, they need to be engaged in activities that propel them forward, piece by piece. Coming to terms with unemployment or redundancy should not be about feeling sorry for yourself and telling everyone about the injustice of the situation, but about sharing skills, time and energy, encouraging others and creating workpieces with them.

This is the opposite scenario to the BBC programme *The Apprentice* with Lord Sugar, which takes a group of people, gives them tasks to perform and every week tells one of them 'You're fired!' until the last man or woman standing gets the job.

Work It Out! apprentices learn together and work together. We're not competing for one job, we're finding workpieces for all of us. There is no shortage of work, but there is a need to go out and gather it into workpieces.

Rather than being glad to see each person leave the team because it means getting closer to securing the one and only job, we want to keep everyone in the team because we recognize we need all the help, support and experience we can get.

MAKE SURE YOU'RE QUALIFIED FOR THE NEW WORLD OF WORK

Qualifications used to be the key for getting a job, but more and more it's experience and capability that matter. The questions an employer will ask are: Can this person deliver? and What is the quality of their work?

In the old world of work, qualifications were the adornments that employers looked for when deciding about a candidate's suitability for work. In Work It Out!, qualifications exist for our own benefit. They are the benchmarks that show we have the skills, insights and concepts to navigate our way through the new world of work and achieve self-sustainability.

GOVERNMENT LEVERAGE

What can governments do at a national level to enable individuals to take more responsibility for their own futures?

- A Work It Out! section should be set up and there should be an appraisal of the implications and possibilities of Work It Out! across all departments.

- Local and central government should review recruitment policies with the aim of becoming much more inclusive. Available work should be not be parcelled up as traditional full-time jobs, but as a number of workpieces. One job could now be three workpieces, for example.

- The tax system should provide specific incentives for individuals to build their own pension (passive income) from workpieces.

- Likewise there should be specific tax incentives for those who create workpieces for others, for example for companies who create part-time Work It Out! workpieces for people confined to their homes.

- There should be an awards scheme for Work It Out! best-practice ideas and successes that others can learn from.

- There needs to be a thorough reform of the way that benefits are paid to people out of work. At the moment, for instance, anyone claiming Jobseeker's Allowance who has the opportunity to do some casual work and earns a small amount of money, loses their benefit. This makes it very difficult for the unemployed to start making money from workpieces. It forces them back on the all-or-nothing of full-time job or unemployment, rather than allowing them to build up their income in increments as workpieces are created and delivered.

Current policy makes it very difficult for people to become self-sustaining – they are either dependent on benefits, or dependent on keeping a full-time job.

TOWARDS THE END OF UNEMPLOYMENT

Within Work It Out! there is no such notion as unemployment. There is always plenty of work to be done in businesses, our families, in our communities and across the world. All of us have skills and experiences we can use and share to make life better for others, create our new workpieces and build our futures.

Rather than setting people up by telling them to find that big job and keeping them waiting for benefits to arrive each week, it would make more sense to reward them as Work It Out! workers. They should be encouraged and supported through structured initiatives to start developing workpieces. Government financial support should be used as starter funds to get people up and running, and as a reward for their efforts.

Jobseekers Allowance or other unemployment benefits should be transformed into funding for an unemployed individual's first workpiece. This money would provide a financial headstart – a free funded workpiece from the Government to pay for learning about Work It Out!

It just does not make sense to have young people sitting around with little to do, or experienced managers not being able to use their skills. Funds that are being spent on benefits could be used to bring people together. Work would get done, people would learn to create their own workpieces and support each other, and the Government would save money. The old world of benefits could be replaced by a more positive Work It Out! training allowance. This would become the first income workpiece, and a framework upon which to build other workpieces. The expectation within Work It Out! is that within six months individuals will have made progress towards self-sustainability and then become a net contributor to the economy.

CHAPTER 11

Work It Out!: A Way of Life

This chapter takes a step back to consider the overall philosophy and potential influence of Work It Out!, showing how it can be applied to help you shape the future you want. It also places Work It Out! in the context of cooperating with people in our local communities and in the wider world.

At its core, Work It Out! is about sustainability, which is the most important attribute of any system for dealing with the new realities of work.

CASE STUDY: KATHY

Kathy, a qualified boiler engineer, was made redundant as a result of a merger. For the first time in her life she had to receive unemployment benefit, and was struggling to meet the needs of her two young children. She applied for numerous jobs, but was not even offered an interview. Not surprisingly, Kathy became disillusioned and dispirited. Last September, Karina, a friend on Facebook, suggested that she should look at Work It Out!

Inspired by the inquisitive nature of her children, then aged three and four, and using her own engineering knowledge, Kathy decided to create a couple of fun science games for the under-fives. Other parents helped to test the ideas and within eight weeks Kathy had her first 'fun kit' and her 'Kathy and the Scientists' website. Robbie, whom she met through Work It Out!, helped her to set up an e-commerce shop, and by week 13 Kathy had received the first online orders for her 'Kathy and the Scientists Fun Kits'.

Parents with older children asked Kathy if she could help with science tuition for older kids at weekends, and so her second workpiece was created. One friend, Stephanie, agreed to swap some childcare hours for Kathy's children in return for free tutoring for her son.

Kathy has started to build her future with workpieces that meet the needs of her young children and her own development. Her online and local community networks have grown also to offer friendship, support and ideas.

AN INCLUSIVE GLOBAL PERSPECTIVE

Work It Out! recognizes that our lives have to be firmly rooted in an approach which is cooperative, mutually supportive and fully inclusive. In an interconnected world, this not only refers to the people in our network or our local community: we have to take account of the needy and starving wherever they are. It is no longer enough for us as individuals to look after our own financial needs, or as nations just to be concerned about our own economies.

This is not altruism, philanthropy or corporate social responsibility. It is not a token approach, or something designed to help us feel better about ourselves. Rather, it is the absolute core requirement of a system that will be robust, embracing and sustainable, one that is capable of dealing with the grand challenges coming our way, from global pandemics, climate change, energy security, population growth and ageing to the burden of chronic disease, human migration and natural disasters.

It may seem we have come a long way from the starting point of how to get a job. But then life in the mill was a whole new world for the traditional farmhand. Work It Out! sets up a framework and provides us with the tools for living in a rapidly changing and interdependent world.

BUILD YOUR WORLDWIDE NETWORK WITH WORK IT OUT!

The new world of Work It Out! is enabled by modern communications. We can link up with almost anyone in the world via email, find new friends on social networking websites and find people to help us with different parts of our work though a host of websites where people are buying and selling services.

Finding others to help and accessing the skills we need has never been easier. There is a worldwide resource to help in building workpieces.

Ask yourself:

- What are the skills, expertise, inputs and support that I need on each workpiece to push it forward?

- How can I use my email network to help in each workpiece?

- How can I use my social networking friends to help?

- How can I use freelance websites to pull in additional skills as needed?

Try and be clear which workpieces are central to taking you forward in the right direction. What is working for you? These are the workpieces to strengthen.

WORK IT OUT! PERSONAL ASSESSMENT

- Have I identified what I really want to do?

- Have I written down a description of a workpiece that would help me to progress in this direction?

- Have I created a plan with the activities or steps that need to happen, with a timetable for when I will do them?

- Have I been able to identify other skills, experience, knowledge or support I need for this workpiece which I don't have?

- Have I been able to find another person(s) who can provide these skills, experience, knowledge or support?

- Have I started to build this workpiece?

- Have I reviewed where I am with this every day, reminding myself of why it is important and being determined to take the next step forward?

- Have I helped others with their workpieces?

- Have I got a range of workpieces I am working on?

- Am I moving closer to what I really want to do?

MY WORK IT OUT!

Finally, it would be great to hear your Work It Out! story and how you are creating and piecing together the life that you want. Drop me a note at equalitytraining@aol.com as soon as you can. Thanks.

> For further information on Work It Out! training programmes and support materials, please visit Des McCabe's website on personal development:
>
> www.Great-Quotes-On-Life.com
>
> Des McCabe is a popular conference speaker and can be contacted at:
>
> equalitytraining@aol.com

Index

NOTES

NOTES

NOTES

NOTES

Hay House titles of related interest

Effortless Success (CD),
by Michael Neill

How to Become a Money Magnet,
by Marie-Claire Carlyle

Just Get On With It!,
by Ali Campbell

Success Intelligence,
by Robert Holden

You Can Have What You Want,
by Michael Neill

JOIN THE HAY HOUSE FAMILY

As the leading self-help, mind, body and spirit publisher in the UK, we'd like to welcome you to our family so that you can enjoy all the benefits our website has to offer.

 EXTRACTS from a selection of your favourite author titles

 COMPETITIONS, PRIZES & SPECIAL OFFERS Win extracts, money off, downloads and so much more

 LISTEN to a range of radio interviews and our latest audio publications

 CELEBRATE YOUR BIRTHDAY An inspiring gift will be sent your way

 LATEST NEWS Keep up with the latest news from and about our authors

 ATTEND OUR AUTHOR EVENTS Be the first to hear about our author events

 **iPHONE APPS** Download your favourite app for your iPhone

 HAY HOUSE INFORMATION Ask us anything, all enquiries answered

join us online at **www.hayhouse.co.uk**

  292B Kensal Road, London W10 5BE
T: 020 8962 1230 E: info@hayhouse.co.uk

ABOUT THE AUTHOR

 **Des McCabe** is one of the UK's leading experts on human resource management and workplace training. After a number of corporate roles, in 1984 he founded The Training Business, which in the 1980s and early 1990s grew to become the largest independent training organization in the UK. By the time the company was sold in 1995 it was finding jobs for 5,000 long-term unemployed and helping 4,000 people to get qualifications every year.

Des's expertise in the field of job creation led to him becoming an advisor to the British, Irish, US, Argentinian, Romanian and Albanian governments on employment, social inclusion and training-related policy. He received formal recognition of his standing as one of the leading job-creation entrepreneurs from 'Europe's 500', one of Europe's most prominent bodies of entrepreneurs.

Beyond his professional achievements, Des established and raised funding for The Training Trust, an international charity set up to meet the humanitarian needs of children in Romanian orphanages. In Africa, Des has been involved in Comic Relief projects in Kenya, and has supported a range of anti-poverty work in Ghana and Madagascar. Closer to home, he was an advisor to the Irish and US governments in the early stages of the Northern Ireland Peace Process.

Over the past two years, Des has been leading the formulation and development of *Work It Out!* as a response to the new realities of work in the globalized Internet age. He himself is a *Work It Out!* worker, and with his colleagues he provides advice and support to individuals, organizations and governments on how to *Work It Out!*